THE STRATEGIC MVP

THE
STRATEGIC
MVP

52 Growth & Leadership Tools from the World's Top Executives

MARK THOMPSON AND BRANDI STANKOVIC

ACKNOWLEDGEMENTS

This book is a collaborative effort harvesting the hearts and minds of our mentors, clients, family, and friends. Thank you to all who contributed. We would like to express particular gratitude to our coaching partner, Marshall Goldsmith, who inspired many of these exercises; along with Brian Tracy, coauthor for *Now Build a Great Business*; and Bonita Thompson, coauthor of New York Times bestseller, *Admired: 21 Ways to Double Your Value*. We would also like to give a shout out to 99designs for an innovative approach to our cover design; Mitchell, Stankovic & Associates; Southwest Strategic; and all the colleagues who dedicated their late nights, as only MVPs would.

CONTENTS

THE STRATEGIC MVP

FOREWORD
BY MARSHALL GOLDSMITH

What you have in your hands, The Strategic MVP, was inspired by my friend Peter Drucker, who once shared with us a simple truth about leadership: The job of a leader is to recruit and develop other leaders. What that means for you today as a manager is that you must strive to become the best coach you can be, whether you are coordinating the efforts of a small team or driving the collaboration of a multinational corporation.

With that in mind, Mark, Brandi, and I reviewed 30 years of our work in the field of executive coaching to find our favorite team exercises. We looked at what is relevant in today's swiftly changing environment and created concepts for you to practically integrate into your daily regime. In addition, we have added thoughts from many of our clients who are among the world's top CEOs. Many of them are household names, including Elizabeth Smith, Warren Buffett, Maya Hu-Chan, Jim Collins, Charles Schwab, Sir Richard Branson, and our new partner, Alan Mulally. Each of these experienced executives generously shared with us their insights across the landscape of leadership, from personal improvement or best hiring practices to advice on how to focus on the most meaningful priorities.

In all, we assembled 52 exercises – one for every week – in a simple format that enables you to build your leadership mojo throughout the year. Too many leadership and coaching books settle on telling you what to do or what worked for others. As our friend Jim Collins would say: This workbook is meant to be put to work! It is designed for you and your team to do the practical work necessary to take your team from good to great despite all odds—to become the best you can be.

College basketball legend John Wooden won 10 national championships in 12 years while he was coaching at UCLA, which was unprecedented; and no coach has come close to that level in the 40 years since he retired. But Wooden did not define success by wins, or by championships, or by how many of his players went on to glory in the National Basketball Association. Instead, Wooden said simply: "Success is peace of mind, which is a direct result of self-satisfaction in knowing you made the effort to do your best to become the best that you are capable of becoming."

It is our hope that you use these simple exercises to challenge yourself and others to take your game to the next level, to reach your greater potential, and to become the MVP that you deserve to be.

INTRODUCTION

Leadership...it is likely the most researched and communicated topic in business, and yet questions have persisted for decades about exactly what it is, who has it, and how to achieve it. What exactly does *leadership* mean? Is it something you *do* or something you *have*? Is it something that you are born with or something that can be learned? If so, what approach to learning is the most effective? Who does it best? Oops, who does it best *now* (since last year's best example is often disrupted and overtaken by next year's winner)? What will work tomorrow when everything in business changes again?

At the same time, leadership is more personal than ever, isn't it? Your commitment to 50-70 hour workweeks means that what you do each day during your career often ends up defining the biggest part of your life. What we have found in three decades of research is that the only way to survive and prosper under these circumstances is to commit to *continual growth* in ways that ignite your passions, focusing your energy and executing on meaningful ways to realize your dreams. Ultimately, from an organizational and personal perspective, *a leader is someone who defines what matters*. A leader is someone who can win support for a compelling vision with a team that will collectively rally to a cause and manifest that destiny.

To help you accelerate the development of your strategic leadership skills, we have simplified the learning process for you by compiling winning strategies from the top leadership researchers, coaches, and professionals in the business. For the purposes of this book, we closely examined the journey that we embarked on with each of our executive coaching clients as we facilitated their personal and professional development. We collected our top exercises and lessons from decades of experience, both working with great leaders and also coaching emerging leaders from every corner of the globe and in organizations from startups to Fortune 100 companies. We road-tested these exercises for 30 years with the world's most successful businesspeople in a myriad of industries to provide a fresh perspective on the application of our tools.

This book is intended for an all-star, an MVP, a person who is hungry for the next level of growth. When we hear the term "MVP", it inevitably conjures up visions of sports, and the top athletes who have that something extra, the magic stuff or mojo that drives them not only to achieve personal success – but also to help lift an entire team to win games, championships, or Olympic medals. In business, we refer to MVPs as our top performers; the ones who impact the bottom line or who can turn around a low-performing team and help them achieve their goals and exceed their targets. In our personal lives, our MVPs are those who contribute, in a tangible way, to our success and well-being every day – they might be our parents, best friends, spouses, children, or teachers. Whatever the frame of reference, MVPs are the people who have the courage to make the choice to get better every day; to achieve their objectives and live life in a meaningful way. **MVPs are the people** who inspire others to achieve success.

In sports, even the most gifted professional athletes focus attention on their technique and fundamentals and work with coaches who help them continuously hone their skills and strategies. Name any sport – the world's top runners, golfers, swimmers, baseball players, and footballers still work out with coaches on a daily basis. Many of the best have more than one coach – those who work on the strength and stamina for the physical game and those who work on strategy, focus, and the mental tenacity required to win. Coaches keep the top-achieving athletes at the height of their game.

In business, it is no different – the most visionary business leaders seek advice and information from trusted outside sources to inform their decisions, to help them learn, grow, and gain perspective that they might not otherwise receive from internal peers, bosses, or employees. It is critical to have an advisor or small group of advisors who ask tough questions to push you out of your comfort zone and to help you grow regardless of whether you are an entry level employee or next in line for the corner office (or even when you are already there). In the wise words of Pitbull, "Ask for money? Get advice. Ask for advice? Get money twice." Ok, maybe the words are not that wise, but the underlying notion of the value of growth through coaching is.

In this book, we are focused on people – the **MOST VALUABLE PEOPLE** – specifically you and how to be an MVP and how to inspire the MVPs in your life. The Strategic MVP is a book of exercises that will inspire you to go all out and reach your destination, but requires you to dig deeply and to engage in the process in order to fulfill your potential. There are 52 exercises that can be utilized for your own personal development or for helping coach your next in command. In each chapter, you will be given **The Play:** an overview of the coaching exercise with **Required Action**. Then you will review the **Outcome** to evaluate your actions and to determine if you have met the purpose. Many of the exercises in this book are focused on personal growth – while others will stretch your leadership skills as a valued member of a team or when leading one.

Think through the exercises to create your own personal plan. Think big. Close Your Eyes. Dream. Your journey begins with your executive coach asking you to reflect upon your dreams, identify what you love, and unleash your passion and energy.

SECTION I — YOUR LEADERSHIP PROFORMA

The only place success comes before work is in the dictionary. -Vince Lombardi

In Section I of our Strategic MVP, we are going to take an analytical and strategic approach to developing your leadership skills as if we were creating a personal business plan for you. When building a new business or venture, investors require executives to do research, know the market, understand the marketing strategy, set financial goals, and analyze the competitors. If we utilize this approach for your leadership, we can ensure that the proper diligence is done and the right questions are asked. Section I will guide you through developing your personal leadership proforma, or the projection of your success.

Take a moment to think - if you could redesign your vision or life, how would you approach it? Where can you provide value? Imagine yourself as the Most Valuable Person. How would an organization benefit from having you on the team? How would your customers build value in their lives by having you around? Throughout this section, we will help you to find your voice and fine tune your own personal value proposition. The more opportunities and reasons an organization has to promote/hire/recruit/retain you, the broader your path to success—and the more you will be seen as an indispensable MVP!

Remember, every exercise within the Strategic MVP can be utilized for your personal leadership journey as well as a guide to help you coach your team.

SKETCH YOUR SWOT

The people in my songs are all me. -Bob Dylan

The Play

As you begin your leadership journey, it is important to know your starting point, the foundation upon which you will build your future. Your personal SWOT analysis is a way to determine where you are today - your strengths, weaknesses, opportunities, and threats. This exercise will help you to assess yourself and your environment.

Required Action

Describe your top three thoughts in each category of the SWOT analysis:

Strengths: The things that come naturally to you, your talents or what you have achieved such as your education, your experience, or your attitude.

_____

_____

Weaknesses: You often spend most of your time working on being better, rather than focusing on your talents. What do you consider your natural weaknesses, things that you worry about that might get in your way?

_____

_____

Opportunities: As you consider the future, what are the top three things that you may be able take advantage of based upon your current situation?

_____

_____

Threats: Are you confronting important issues that may threaten your success? What things should you consider as you move forward through the Strategic MVP?

_____

_____

Outcome

You identified the sources of your achievements and challenges, and now you can begin a journey through this book that will help you turn your weaknesses into opportunities. Creating a starting point or foundation is essential to manage growth. You will review the importance of measurement in managing results throughout this book, and you will refer back to this SWOT analysis at the end of the Strategic MVP book to see if the situation has changed.

DISCOVER YOUR MOJO

We are all stars and we deserve to twinkle. -Marilyn Monroe

THE PLAY

Before you set a goal, it is best to find your mojo. One important ingredient to discover your own mojo is to know your identity. Who are you today? Who were you 10 years ago? Who is the person you want to be tomorrow? This exercise will build on your personal SWOT and ask you to examine your identity.

REQUIRED ACTION

Using the spaces provided below, answer the following questions as you seek to learn and understand your identity:

How do you view your past? What experiences do you remember that make you who you are today?

_____

_____

What have other people in your past said about you?

_____

_____

Is this the person you would like to continue to be? Why or why not?

_____

_____

_____

_____

If not, who is the person you would like to be? Describe this person.

_____

_____

_____

_____

OUTCOME

You find your mojo in the moment you do something so purposeful, powerful, and positive that it is easier to see your enthusiasm and energy in the mirror. Throughout this book, you will be helping to build your mojo by identifying what turns you on and what makes you more authentic in everything you do. If you want to change, you are the ONLY person who can make that happen. You need to believe you can and make the courageous choices necessary to be that person. Feed your mojo, and you will be on track to becoming an MVP.

WARREN BUFFETT

Warren Buffett sat down with us to discuss his advice to aspiring managers. The CEO of Berkshire Hathaway, famous for his claim that he "tap dances to work," told us that the difference between becoming a good leader and a great one is a matter of finding your mojo. Everyone around you can tell if you're "happy where you're working," Buffett smirked. "I always worry about people who say, I'm going to do this for 10 years, and I don't like it very well. How does that make everyone around you feel?" The legendary investor thinks that your sour attitude is not only bad for the culture; it undermines your creative energy and enthusiasm. Putting off your passions is "a little like saving up sex for your old age. Not a good idea!"

Notes:

FINE-TUNE YOUR PROFESSIONAL MOJO

Absorb what is useful, discard what is not, add what is uniquely your own. -Bruce Lee

THE PLAY

Now that you have started to more deeply explore your personal mojo, let's discuss your professional mojo. How does your personal identity transfer into your career choices? Do you have mojo with your colleagues and peers? What are you doing to develop a clear identity that your clients and team can grasp?

REQUIRED ACTION

Using the spaces provided below, answer the following questions:

Am I motivated to do my job? Why or why not?

_____

_____

_____

_____

Do I have the ability to do the job?

_____

_____

_____

_____

Do I know what to do and how to do it? What one skill or resource do I need to improve my competency?

_____

_____

How do I measure my skills at work?

_____

_____

What action can I take each week to be better at my job?

_____

_____

OUTCOME

You have taken the first important step to outline your professional mojo. It is not easy, but it is well worth the investment to analyze what it is that makes you feel motivated, capable, knowledgeable, confident, and authentic.

IDENTIFY WHO YOU ADMIRE

I admire work, dedication and competence. -Ayrton Senna

THE PLAY

Great leaders have role models who have inspired them to be more and do more than they originally imagined was possible. Ask your boss, your peers, and your team who they admire, and you will hear them describe emotional moments filled with insights into what they really care about. From our coaching process, you have learned that the people you admire are a reflection of what you value and what matters to you. In fact, asking anyone who they admire is a great way to understand more about who they are in an unthreatening or noninvasive way. At the same time, the fact that you inquired is so flattering that those same folks will appreciate you more for having asked them. What you admire in others reveals something about who and what you aspire to become as a leader. One of the most important roles of a leader is to identify the qualities you admire in others by putting them into practice on a daily basis. Take the time today to think about how those traits would improve your life and work. As Gandhi said, *Be the change you wish to see*. Admiration does not happen by accident!

REQUIRED ACTION

Who are three people you most admire in your life or work, and list three reasons why.

Name of Person: _____

    1

    2

    3

Name of Person: _____

    1

    2

    3

Name of Person: _____

    1

    2

    3

Circle any qualities that appear in more than one of the individuals listed above.

Which traits do you want to embrace? Why?

_____

_____

_____

_____

Complete the same exercise with your boss and team to identify what qualities define the leaders they most admire and why.

OUTCOME

Asking who you admire strikes at the heart of what you—and the people most important to you—really value without any obligation to be politically correct. It is easy to ask, but harder to implement in your life. The question now is how will you put those qualities you admire most into practice.

JIM COLLINS

Jim Collins, author and co-author of six books that have sold more than ten million copies worldwide, believes aspiring leaders should continue to learn from others. He shared with us, "Level 5 leaders have a brilliant combination of humility and hubris—the humility to know that nothing gets done **alone**—that everything worthwhile is accomplished only when you recruit other people to the cause or to your team. And nothing gets done unless you have the humility to learn from others." Collins believes that every leader has something to learn. Combine eagerness to learn with a confidence to succeed and a leader can accomplish anything. "I've never met an Olympian who didn't believe they could do better next time."

CULTIVATE YOUR PERSONAL BRAND

Your brand is what people say about you when you're not in the room. -Jeff Bezos

THE PLAY

Similar to the brand of a company, your personal brand is the feeling and experience that people have when they interact with you, think about you, or talk about you. Do you have an identifiable personal brand? Managing your personal brand can be one of the most important things you do as you progress in business. What do you want to be known for? If your personal brand is authentically focused on your career aspirations, then the right people will think of YOU when the right opportunity arises. Your personal brand should articulate your values, story, message, and things that are important to you. Let's examine how you project this brand to others.

REQUIRED ACTION

Write down four words that describe you...in 30 seconds or less. Go!

1
2
3
4

Now, ask three different people to send you four words that describe you in 30 seconds or less. Try to select personal and professional contacts, superiors, or direct reports, allowing for diversity in your feedback. You are not attempting to conduct a 360-degree feedback here; you are more attempting to collect perspective on how people perceive you. Once you have the observations collected, consider the following things:

Are the characteristics different than how you described yourself? If so, how?

_____

_____

Do you like the way they described you? Is this what experience you want them to have with you?

_____

_____

Do the characteristics differ in regards to intensity? (Did you think you are outgoing and they said gregarious? Assertive vs aggressive?)

_____

_____

Describe the person you would like to be. Use the discoveries you made in your Mojo and Admired exercises.

_____

_____

What 5 steps do you need to take to better manage your brand?

1

2

3

4

5

OUTCOME

Your personal brand is an important part of your MVP leadership journey and the key to your long-term success. Now, build upon those characteristics and be consistent in your efforts and message. You may have to reinvent yourself along the way to stay relevant.

LYNDA GRATTON

Lynda Gratton is one of the world authorities on people in organizations and a Professor of Management Practice at London Business School. She is the author of *Glow: How You Can Radiate Energy, Innovation and Success* and *Hot Spots: Why Some Teams, Workplaces, and Organizations Buzz with Energy – And Others Don't*, and most recently, *The Shift – The Future of Work is Already Here*. She recently shared, "I believe that in the future the means by which individual value is created will shift from having generalist ability to having specialist ability and achieving serial mastery. Why? Because if you remain a generalist, there are thousands, perhaps even millions, of people who can do the same work as you do – yet faster, cheaper and perhaps even better. In the future you will have to differentiate yourself from the crowd, build depth yet be prepared to shift gears across the course of your working life." She noted that refining your personal brand can help you differentiate.

CONCEPTUALIZE THE FUTURE

You will see it when you believe it, not the other way around. -Wayne Dyer

THE PLAY

Successful people have a continuous focus on the future. They think about how the future will change and how they can be a driving force in that transformation. To create or idealize success, think about how the great men and women of the ages have thought about and have achieved success. Did they create opportunity through adversity and humble beginnings? Their success stemmed from believing, thinking, and knowing they COULD succeed.

REQUIRED ACTION

Imagine that you have a magic wand that allows you to create any future you desire. How would it be different from today? Use the space below to write your answer, and be as specific as you can.

_____

_____

_____

_____

Now, if you were earning your ideal income, in your dream job, with focused and success-driven team members, what would it look like? How would it be different from today? Use the space below to write your answer.

_____

_____

_____

_____

What three steps could you take in the coming months to build a few of those characteristics into your life and work?

    1
    2
    3

OUTCOME

Think about how the people you admire most have built a life that matters. Their success stemmed from believing, thinking, and knowing they could succeed, and recruiting others to join that adventure.

IGNITE YOUR PASSION

You have to be burning with an idea, or a problem, or a wrong that you want to right.
If you're not passionate enough from the start, you'll never stick it out. -Steve Jobs

THE PLAY

Passionate people work tirelessly to achieve their goals and ultimately, are happier people. In the office, passion generates productivity, creativity, and innovation. These people are paid more, but they are also worth more. Are you doing something you are passionate about? Do you know what your passion is? Let's spend some time reviewing what creates your passion; it may surprise you. There are six fundamental factors that determine when passion is present.

REQUIRED ACTION

In each of the areas below, think about the impact on your passion and answer the question.

1. Flow: What is it that you are doing or thinking about most when you lose track of time? Social scientist Mihaly Csikszentmihalyi studied the success of some of the most accomplished and happy people. He asked, "What makes a life worth living?" Noting that money cannot make us happy, he looked to those who find pleasure and lasting satisfaction in activities that bring about a state of "flow."

_____

_____

_____

2. Failure: What is it that you do not mind doing even if you fail? People tend to define things they do not like as failure when it does not go well. But people who love doing something usually define those same difficult times as setbacks or learning!

_____

_____

_____

3. Free: What is one thing you would do (at least secretly) for free? What is it that makes you go above and beyond what is required, so you are not so concerned about how much time or energy you have expended?

_____

_____

_____

4. Distraction: What distracts you on a regular basis? Rather than avoid its pull, perhaps you should be paying more attention to it and doing more! Notice this also in the people you care about to see if you can direct that energy rather than avoid it.

_____

_____

_____

5. Unpopular: Is there something you like to do even if you are not that great at it and it is not popular with other people? When you are engaged in a passion, you tend to get lost in the pleasure of the experience and become generally less self-conscious or aware of needing to be politically correct.

_____

_____

_____

6. Irritation: What really annoys you when you see it done poorly by others? It would not bother you so much if it was not important to you to see it done well!

_____

_____

_____

Now, take a look at your answers and circle any of them that appear more than once. *Is that your passion? Do this same exercise with the members of your team to learn more about how to motivate them, or rather, to direct their efforts toward activities in which they are more self-motivated.*

OUTCOME

It is important to examine both our ideals and our irritants in order to ignite our passions. Listen carefully as your reactions and emotions may lead you to your passion! Passion is one thing that all high achievers have in common, and to become a long-term performer, you must embrace it if you want to reach greatness.

DEVIN WENIG

Igniting your passion refreshes your purpose. Before you bury yourself in all the minutiae of planning or setting goals, ask an existential question about why you do what you do. Just three years after arriving at eBay, Devin Wenig was promoted to CEO to lead a historic new chapter for that company. His advice for leaders, "As you plunge into all the important issues of administration, capital, and systems necessary to keep your business running, you have to stay grounded in the only major reason you and your company exist: To deliver better experiences for your customers than your competitors!" Wenig smiled and leaned on the conference table in his scrappy Silicon Valley office. "You have to start and finish every day focused on how you're creating greater engagement in a world where people have endless choices and distractions." Understanding your purpose and passion will energize your efforts and every single person you touch.

ACHIEVE

If a window of opportunity appears, don't pull the shades. -Tom Peters

THE PLAY

Determining a goal and writing it down may be simple; however, the task of achieving it often seems daunting and may stop a person from completing the tasks. Below is a seven-step process for achieving goals you can use the rest of your life. You will go through this process in detail so you can create your strategy for each goal you have set for yourself.

REQUIRED ACTION

Using the following steps, you will define a goal and create a strategy for each of your goals. Take a look at what you will need to do:

1. **Make it measurable.** Decide exactly what you want. Be specific, and make it measurable. Your goal should be so clear that a 10-year-old child could tell you how close you are to achieving it.
2. **Write it down.** Give it concrete form. You have already done this! It is important to note that people with written goals are 10 times more likely to complete them.
3. **Set a deadline.** You need a target to aim at if you want to achieve your goal. If your goal is big enough, set sub-deadlines as well.
4. **Make a list of tasks.** List everything you can think of that you could possibly do to achieve your goal. As you think of new tasks and activities, write them down until your list is complete.
5. **Prioritize.** Organize the list by both sequence and priority. Arrange your list in the right sequence by determining what you will have to do first, before you move on to something else. Organize your list by priority by determining what is more important and what is less important. Now you have a plan!
6. **Take action on your plan immediately.** Do something. Do anything. Step out in faith. Think of anything that motivates you to take action. The very act of taking action on your goal begins a mental and an emotional process that can transform your life.
7. **Make daily progress.** Do something every day that moves you forward. Seven days a week, 365 days a year, do something, anything that moves you a little bit in the right direction. Small moves matter. This sense of forward momentum will energize and empower you and will eventually make you unstoppable and irresistible.

Use the following pages. Write each goal and put it in priority order. Then, answer the questions and start moving forward! Extra achieve pages are available at the end of the book if needed.

OUTCOME

All successful people are intensely action-oriented. They are in constant motion. They try, try again, and then try something else. They believe in "doing it, fixing it, and trying it." The fact is, the more actions you take in the direction of your goals, the greater probability that you will achieve the goal.

ACHIEVE

GOAL: _____

PRIORITY #

What is the measurement?

_____

_____

_____

_____

What is my deadline to achieve this goal?

_____

_____

_____

_____

What will I need to do to accomplish this goal?

1

2

3

4

5

When am I going to start this goal?

_____

_____

_____

_____

How will I keep this goal in the forefront so I will remember to focus on it every day?

_____

_____

_____

_____

ACHIEVE

GOAL: _____

PRIORITY #

What is the measurement?

_____
_____
_____
_____

What is my deadline to achieve this goal?

_____
_____
_____
_____

What will I need to do to accomplish this goal?

1
2
3
4
5

When am I going to start this goal?

_____
_____
_____
_____

How will I keep this goal in the forefront so I will remember to focus on it every day?

_____
_____
_____
_____

ACHIEVE

GOAL: _____

PRIORITY #

What is the measurement?

_____

_____

_____

_____

What is my deadline to achieve this goal?

_____

_____

_____

_____

What will I need to do to accomplish this goal?

1

2

3

4

5

When am I going to start this goal?

_____

_____

_____

_____

How will I keep this goal in the forefront so I will remember to focus on it every day?

_____

_____

_____

_____

ACHIEVE

GOAL: _____

PRIORITY #

What is the measurement?

_____
_____
_____
_____

What is my deadline to achieve this goal?

_____
_____
_____
_____

What will I need to do to accomplish this goal?

    1
    2
    3
    4
    5

When am I going to start this goal?

_____
_____
_____
_____

How will I keep this goal in the forefront so I will remember to focus on it every day?

_____
_____
_____
_____

PRIORITIZE

The art of leadership is saying no, not yes. It is very easy to say yes. -Tony Blair

THE PLAY

Now that you have defined your goals to enhance all areas of your life as a MVP, you will be focusing on what matters most. This step is critical to the positive development in your career and forward progression.

REQUIRED ACTION

Review the goals you have created over the past few exercises. What one goal, if you could accomplish it in 24 hours, would have the greatest positive impact on your life?

_____

_____

_____

_____

Why?

_____

_____

_____

_____

Go back and highlight those goals in the previous exercise that are most important to your growth.

OUTCOME

Prioritize to maintain a laser focus on what you want. This exercise should be implemented as a best practice across all goals, daily tasks, and future expectations. There is a seven-step process for achieving goals like this one that you can use for the rest of your life. This process will be highlighted in the next exercise.

LEARN FROM LEADERS

Great leaders are like the best conductors - they reach beyond the notes to the magic in the players. -Blaine Lee

THE PLAY

Once you are clear about where you are heading, it is easier to break down a series of steps to get there faster and more effectively. One of the best ways to do that is to better understand how the best people arrived at the destination you are heading. In this exercise, you will visualize and identify the top people in the field or industry you aspire to master, and if possible, take steps to meet them.

REQUIRED ACTION

Who are four or more leaders in your desired field or profession who define the life and career you would like to build over the long term? You may want to revisit your Identify Who You Admire exercise list.

1

2

3

4

What could you read about them or by them that would help you determine the steps you could take on your journey?

_____

_____

_____

_____

Is there any way possible to meet any of these leaders?   **YES NO**

If your answer is No, consider what non-profit activities and personal hobbies they may have that would enable you to see them in action doing something they are doing out of generosity or passion.

_____

_____

_____

_____

List those organizations or activities below, and plan to attend events or meetings where the people who run those organizations gather on a regular basis.

_____

_____

_____

_____

OUTCOME

Discovering people who are living your dream and have accomplished similar goals will help translate your vision to reality. Emulate their efforts. Seek leaders as mentors. Work alongside like-minded leaders. Implement strategies that are known to work. Build your influence. Highly accomplished leaders have lessons or methods that facilitated their success. Learn from these leaders.

RUTH ANN HARNISCH

"I work every day to apply my money and my moxie to the biggest problem in the world - untapped capacity. In my coaching, my grant making, and my donor activities and organizations, I want to help people discover how much they've got and how to make the most of it for themselves and for others," stated Ruth Ann Harnisch, President of the Harnisch Foundation. Harnisch believes there is something to learn from all leaders. Her foundation funds innovations in coaching, journalism, and philanthropy. Harnisch is also a founder of the Institute of Coaching at Harvard, the annual International Coaching Research Forum, as well as the Coaching Commons, a worldwide forum for coaching news and commentary. She encourages people to identify those people accomplishing the goals you want to achieve, and discover their philanthropic passions as well. "There is great thrill in learning as well as giving time, skills, ideas and other assets to the causes you care about."

CLARIFY AND CONQUER

*You're better off living what you're for rather than wasting
your days fighting what you're against.* -Bonita Thompson

THE PLAY

Eighty percent of your success in business and in life is going to be determined by the level of clarity you have in your vision and focus. Effective leaders know *exactly* what they are trying to accomplish. Those who report to them are clear about what is expected to achieve the overall goal. Now that you have outlined your goals, take a minute to examine an existing project you are currently working on.

REQUIRED ACTION

Think of a project where you may be experiencing frustration in bringing it to completion. Fill out the information below about that project:

What am I trying to accomplish? (Be specific. If it cannot be measured, it cannot be managed.)

_____

_____

What is my deadline? _____

How am I trying to accomplish it? (Include specific steps, processes, or methodology you are planning to use or are currently using to move you from where you are today to where you want to be.)

_____

_____

_____

_____

How is your method working?

_____

_____

How is it missing the mark, and what resources or support do you need to make it better? What better or alternative ways have been used by your organization or others to accomplish this goal or project?

_____

_____

_____

_____

OUTCOME

The purpose of this exercise is a simple diagnostic to evaluate the clarity of your goal to the progress you are making in its achievement. It is also important to examine how clear your projects and efforts are to you and your team. Can everyone independently articulate precisely the goals, objectives, and measurements for the task? By doing this, you can unearth any existing projects that need greater clarity so that you can combat issues and accelerate your success.

VINOD KUMAR

"The more you can look into why your product or service is being bought, you can defend against your threats." This clarity in mission and service delivery will help expand the organizational knowledge and capacity in the future, says Vinod Kumar. "We can't look at any business as a B2B business or a B2C business. We need to look at a business as a B2B2C or B2B2B or something else." Constantly reimagine and clarify consumer needs as well as the needs of your team to serve them. Vinod Kumar is Managing Director of Tata Communications Limited and CEO of Tata Communications Group, part of the USD $96.8 billion Tata group of companies. He has been at the forefront of Tata Communications' transformation from a traditional connectivity services provider, largely in India, to a global services provider. Kumar believes that clarity is the key to finishing projects, driving growth, and even pushing your organization to the next level.

Notes:

_____

_____

_____

_____

_____

_____

_____

_____

_____

_____

_____

_____

_____

_____

_____

_____

_____

_____

GET OVER IT

The big bad world doesn't owe you a thing...Get over it. -Eagles

THE PLAY

Throughout the previous exercises, you have discussed several strategies to focus on what is important and achieve goals. Now, it is time to free your mind in preparation for the exercises to come. In executive coaching and organizational development, we work with companies all over the world, and in almost every organizational change initiative, restructure, or leadership transition, there is a moment where all people included, even the most evolved ... need to get over it.

Today is a new day, MVP. Yesterday's cultural baggage is from yesterday. People do not want to hear your complaints or what it was like in the good ol' days. Instead, they want to look to the future, and want to know how you will make tomorrow better for them. It is time to move on; however, it is also important to respect the organizational sacred cows and institutionalized approach to systems and processes. Respect tradition, but do not be the person that others have to go around to get things done. Wipe the slate. Get over it.

REQUIRED ACTION

What do you hear yourself whine about? Where do you find yourself easily upset or frustrated?

_____

_____

Any places in life that you find yourself referencing the "way it used to be done"? Why?

_____

_____

Based on the items listed, what do you need to get over? How can you implement this change?

_____

_____

What areas does your staff have baggage they need to get over? How can you help facilitate this change?

_____

OUTCOME

Anticipating your emotional responses can help you combat them. As you build experience and tenure in your career, culture is collected. In some instances, these learnings allow us to focus our efforts and target our results. In other instances, it slows us down. Recognizing areas that you can "get over it" will allow you to focus on what matters. Getting over it is a critical step in building your emotional intelligence as a leader. You are ready to conquer the rest of the Strategic MVP!

SIR RICHARD BRANSON

Sir Richard Branson is the founder and entrepreneurial mastermind behind the 400 companies that carry the Virgin brand. He shared with us the importance of getting over the past. Let your mission define you, not your failures. Branson said that rather than ever feeling threatened or even sorry for himself, he is always comforted by principles shared by his longtime mentor, Nelson Mandela, whose circumstances were obviously far more desperate than any of us will ever experience. "Resentment is like drinking poison and then hoping it will kill your enemies," Mandela once said. Vengefulness and victimhood would not erase the crimes done to him in the past, nor would they help him build a better future. Mandela could have emerged from decades of jail "still imprisoned by bitterness," Branson said. "Instead he devoted every ounce of creativity to building a lasting legacy--just as each of us should during our lifetimes. Get over it and build a great business! You have enduring impact not because you are perfect or lucky," Sir Richard shared, "but because you have the courage to stay focused on building a better future rather than dwell in the past."

Notes:

_____

_____

_____

_____

_____

_____

_____

_____

_____

_____

_____

_____

_____

_____

_____

_____

_____

_____

_____

_____

_____

_____

_____

SECTION II – INDIVIDUAL DEVELOPMENT

Live as if you were to die tomorrow. Learn as if you were to live forever. -Gandhi

The business environment is quickly changing and in order to keep up with the expectations, you must examine your professional needs and aspirations for growth. In the previous section, you envisioned the strategic future and determined your tactical goals, setting the foundation to build your leadership skills. Just like in navigating a business, once the destination is determined, you can research, learn, and create your route to success. In Section II of the Strategic MVP, you will transition into your personal development plan. What will it take to become a MVP, and how can you achieve this next milestone?

There are few opportunities in life to conduct self-evaluation to discover what drives you to succeed. What gives you the greatest sense of accomplishment, self-satisfaction? How do you see yourself growing, and what does that new role look like in the future? These areas can be automatic motivators that you can leverage to achieve greater results. Assessing your current skillset from a technical, interpersonal, and leadership perspective will help you to determine your individual development plan.

We hope to challenge you to step outside of your normal routine of information sharing and education. We want you to enhance your understanding, create new habits of learning, and build your value within your organization. Transform your thoughts into an action plan with realistic steps to increase your effectiveness, enhance your existing talents, and prepare for career development.

CUTLER DAWSON

Cutler Dawson is the CEO of Navy Federal Credit Union, the largest credit union in the world, serving more than 5 million members with 13,000 employees. During his tenure and leadership, the organization has grown from $20B in assets to more than $60B, while continuing to make the Fortune Top Places to Work year after year. Prior to Navy Federal Credit Union, Vice Admiral Dawson served in the U.S. Navy for over 30 years. When we asked about his personal development and leadership success, he stressed the importance of continual learning, requiring his team to know their job, to understand the big picture, and to keep their radar scanning up and down to stay aware of their surroundings. Dawson is also not afraid to ask questions. Upon his arrival to the organization, Dawson asked a 30-year tenured employee, "How can I have the greatest impact?" Dawson believes that continual learning is required to keep an organization and a leader relevant, noting "Loyalty only takes you so far, you have to provide value to people." He urges all leaders to not "retreat to the cabin," a Navy term reflecting the captain returning to the business office on the ship. Some leaders, as they end their careers or build tenure, will assume they know everything, and maintain a been-there-done-that mentality. Dawson shared, "you cannot retreat to the cabin; you must learn and work until the last day you are on the ship."

UNLEASH YOUR INNER NERD

If your culture doesn't like geeks, you are in real trouble. -Bill Gates

THE PLAY

For most, when you are young, your life revolves around school. As kids, learning, growing, and developing is at the center of what you do. Once you get into a career, you might think you can sigh with relief. You are done, phew! In most cases, that is when the journey begins. Learning is a lifelong task in every part of our careers.

REQUIRED ACTION

Answer the following questions:

Is there a degree or a next level of learning that you have been "meaning to do" or a course you have always wanted to accomplish?

_____

_____

Can you take better advantage of the conferences you attend? How are you sharing this knowledge with the rest of the team?

_____

_____

Who do you know that you learn the most from, or with whom you could learn more?

_____

_____

Do you have an outlet for learning and growing? Describe it.

_____

_____

Name one person who can help enhance your learning, or to whom you should connect to learn more.

_____

OUTCOME

Lifelong learning is more than a phrase; it is a commitment to being the best you can be through action, through education, and through learning. Let your inner nerd flourish. This will help you to determine the return on investment for your own personal leadership journey. Embrace education as it allows you to enhance your leadership and position the organization for the future.

JEFF IMMELT

Jeff Immelt is the CEO and Chairman of the board for General Electric, an organization named "America's Most Admired Company" in a poll conducted by Fortune magazine. Immelt was also named one of the "World's Best CEOs" three times by Barron's. We talked with Immelt about the importance of learning for leaders. "The advice I give people is: first get deep and then get broad. Learn something. I started my career and the first 7 or 8 years I was a sales person, manager, marketer, and project manager. I had a trade, skills, and things I could do as well as anyone in the company. And then I got broad." Focusing a portion of time to learning and growth is essential for any leader. You have to want to better yourself, the position, and the organization. Immelt insists that you invest in your skills so that you stand out in every chapter of your career: "My advice is do every job like you are going to have it forever."

Notes:

FEED FORWARD

My attitude is, if someone is going to criticize me, tell me to my face. -Simon Cowell

THE PLAY

In business, leaders commonly use the term "feedback" as a method of engaging in dialogue. The problem with that is that feedback usually devolves into whining about mistakes rather than training people to do it better or giving them opportunities to discover how they might even take their skill to a higher level. You get what you focus on, so the better way to think about this process as a leader is what Marshall Goldsmith coined as Feed Forward. You cannot change the past, but you can be clearer about what success looks like in the future. Feed Forward is a positive, upbeat way to help yourself and others define what success should look like. Feed Forward is based on two key principles:

1. You are not allowed to talk about the past. If you talk about history, then you are not looking forward. Feed Forward focuses on the future and what you can change, not on the past, where you cannot change anything.
2. You cannot judge or critique the ideas that you receive. You must treat each idea as you would a gift. For example, if someone gives you a gift, you would say, "thank you," not throw it to the side. When you receive Feed Forward, you are allowed only to say thanks. To do otherwise reinforces the failure instead of focusing on what you would like to achieve in the future.

REQUIRED ACTION

You will need to ask people for guidance with this exercise. Make sure you are in a location where you can talk to people, such as co-workers, family members, or other trusted people in your life.

Write the following on the top of a piece of paper: "I want to get better at _____." Fill in the blank with any area you would like to improve. Talk to as many people as you can in 5-10 minutes (no more time than that) to get ideas about how you can get better at _____. Tell them to write the ideas on the paper. The more ideas, the better!

What ideas were generated? Capture their thoughts in the space below.

_____

_____

_____

OUTCOME

Feed forward will enhance your effectiveness by focusing on what you are for rather than what you are against. Feed Forward is about helping each other, not judging each other. You need to be open and listen in a non-defensive manner to create a positive future for yourself.

REFLECT ON FEED FORWARD

Leadership and learning are indispensable to each other. -John F. Kennedy

THE PLAY

Let's build on the previous exercise and the fact that Feed Forward is a constructive way to help you and others create a more precise definition of success. Remember, Feed Forward is based on two key principles: You are not allowed to talk about the past; you cannot judge or critique the ideas that you receive.

There are two common misconceptions about giving feedback to others. First, people believe they have to have a deep knowledge about someone in order to provide them with feedback. That is not the case, as you probably found at least a few nuggets of insights during the exercise you just completed. Second, people believe that they have to be better than, or smarter than, someone to provide them with feedback; that is not the case. Our research shows that a fresh perspective from a person outside your field or industry can be rather illuminating.

REQUIRED ACTION

Now that you have been given feedback (or rather, feed forward) from the previous exercise, take some time to really delve into what you learned and how to move forward. What did you learn from this exercise?

_____

_____

_____

_____

Was this exercise more or less painful than the way you have previously received feedback from others?

_____

_____

_____

_____

OUTCOME

You can learn from others and provide feedback based on your own circumstances. Using this process, you are able to see that, in some instances, someone may be working on the exact same issue as you. Now, set up a time where you can work with those you manage, or even with your other co-workers, to do the same Feed Forward exercise you did individually as a team. You will be amazed how much you will gain from this exercise as a team.

COMMUNICATE WITH EMOTIONAL INTELLIGENCE

In a very real sense we have two minds, one that thinks and one that feels. -Daniel Goleman

THE PLAY

Emotional intelligence is a critical component to leadership development. The ability for you to manage and recognize your emotions will help you to better facilitate and empower the emotions of your team. Several of the exercises throughout this book will help you to identify emotions and reactions based on excitement, fear, stress, etc. Today we will examine how your emotions impact your communication. Strong leaders must recognize the impact of emotional intelligence on their social abilities and communication styles. Your awareness and regulation of your own motivation and emotions impact your ability to be effective.

REQUIRED ACTION

What is your communication style? _____

Do you effectively display, relay, communicate emotion authentically? Do people who are close to you feel like they know the real you?

_____

_____

How do you handle anxiety and stress in relation to an urgent goal?

_____

How long does it take you to calm down after an argument or anger? _____

How do you receive criticism? How could you improve?

_____

_____

Revisit the exercise Feed Forward. Utilize this technique to gain feedback from people around you to improve in each of the outlined areas above. What did you learn?

_____

_____

OUTCOME

You recognize your emotions, and you now understand how to improve. Sometimes leaders say things because they want to be heard, rather than to obtain a desired result. Communication is your mechanism to delivering and facilitating the results you want to accomplish, not necessarily an outlet for emotion.

FRAME THE POSITIVE

The best time to plant a tree was 20 years ago. The second best time is now. -Chinese proverb

THE PLAY

Celebrating what is right in the world can be an excruciatingly unhip and uncool thing to do. Many people are carefully trained by safety-conscious parents, institutions of higher learning, and the evening news to ignore or to ridicule optimistic people. In a world rife with violence and generally consumed by fight-or-flight responses, where most people teeter on the verge of being upset or angry, it is hard for people to function when they are not scared or worried. Optimism is a tough pill to swallow, and seems to create an uneasy vacuum that feels almost unrealistic.

REQUIRED ACTION

Let's take a look at a situation you have experienced over the past month when you felt particularly down. Using the space provided, answer the following questions:

How could you have been more optimistic about the situation? Was it possible to turn the negative into a positive? How?

_____

_____

_____

Where do you naturally head – cynicism or optimism? Be as honest with yourself as possible.

_____

_____

_____

Now, what steps can you take to be more optimistic about your life? Your business? Your career?

_____

_____

_____

OUTCOME

Welcome failure as an opportunity to learn. Stay focused on the present, the future, and what it takes to reach your goals. Highly successful people tend to see the benefits of a situation rather than dwell on the negative. These successful people are realistic, but work hard to get to the optimistic view of life as quickly as they can. Do you want to be in charge of creating an exciting and happier place to live? Frame the positive.

SARA BLAKELY

American businesswoman, Sara Blakely, is the founder of Spanx, a multi-million-dollar undergarment company. In 2012, Blakely was named in Time magazine's *Time 100* annual list of the 100 most influential people in the world, and also entered the Forbes list of the world's wealthiest people, as the world's then youngest self-made female billionaire. As of 2014, she is listed as the 93rd most powerful woman in the world by Forbes. "I think failure is nothing more than life's way of nudging you that you are off course. My attitude to failure is not attached to outcome, but in not trying. It is liberating. Most people attach failure to something not working out or how people perceive you. This way, it is about answering to yourself." Failure becomes your opportunity to frame the future in a positive way. Learn from it!

Notes:

BUILD VALUE

Try not to become a man of success, but rather try to become a man of value. -Albert Einstein

THE PLAY

In order to be an MVP at your organization, you must build value. The secret to creating value is to find a mission that speaks to you as a MVP. When you do, you will have more energy and courage to do something that other people value, respect, and eventually, admire. It does not have to be world hunger, but it does have to be personal to you and useful to other people who will hire you or buy your product.

REQUIRED ACTION

Review the four strategies below and reflect on where you need to improve and what opportunities are available.

1. Do Not Try to Be All Things to All People. Be clear about to whom you want to be valuable. How can you help them to define their success and to achieve it?

_____

_____

2. Be Simple, Convenient, and Usable. If you are serving others, are you making it easy to do business with you? Interview your internal stakeholders and customers: Who do you want your target audience to be, do, and/or have. How can you deliver that service better than your competitors, in a way that makes you stand out as the most obvious choice from whom to get help?

_____

_____

3. Showcase What is Valuable. How are you getting the word out about what you do? How are you presenting yourself or your services in a way that makes it attractive to customers?

_____

_____

4. Give a Sense of Security. How can you protect what your target audience believes is valuable? You are generally rewarded by others when you make it clear how hard you will work to defend their interests.

_____

_____

OUTCOME

In this exercise, you took important steps toward identifying your value and how it can impact the organizational mission. Following these strategies will isolate what is meaningful to others and build more value into the product and service you provide.

LAURA WAGNER

"One morning my dad caught found me in the garage after I'd disassembled the lawnmower and taped it to my bicycle. He could have grounded me on the spot, but instead he took me for the ride of my life," Laura Wagner smiled. "I realized that inventions aren't what matters, but how the invention makes you and others feel." Leadership takes heart and soul night and day, so you cannot afford to think about it just as a job or a position of authority. You have to create and build solutions that make a big difference for people and also mean so much to you personally that they get you so excited that you will come roaring back every day no matter what. Laura Wagner is cofounder and CEO of Digitzs—a startup that the media are calling the next PayPal. For decades she has been making a difference in the payments industry.

Notes:

_____
_____
_____
_____
_____
_____
_____
_____
_____
_____
_____
_____
_____
_____
_____
_____
_____
_____
_____
_____
_____
_____
_____
_____
_____

CONTINUE TO BUILD VALUE

I feel that luck is preparation meeting opportunity. -Oprah Winfrey

THE PLAY

There is much required to sustain a value proposition and a long-term reputation. Thinking strategically about the future while embracing the present will help you to achieve your desired outcomes. Reflect upon the final three strategies below and incorporate them with the previous four from the last exercise.

REQUIRED ACTION

Review the additional strategies below that will help you continue to build value. Consider where you need to improve and what opportunities are available.

1. Define Quality. Your stakeholders may define quality differently than you do. Find out how quality is measured by those to whom they must report so that their objective meets that accountability. Describe how they define quality below.

_____

_____

2. Be in the Right Place at the Right Time. To be available to your stakeholders you need to be where they are. Where do you need to spend more time?

_____

_____

3. Dump the Mission Statement. Instead, create a manifesto that is real to your stakeholders and one that you and your team actually believe. Belief in your manifesto will hold your team accountable and will be easier to deliver. Based on all the value statements in this exercise and the previous one, what is your manifesto?

_____

_____

OUTCOME

You have just created a value proposition for yourself and for your work. Come back to this exercise on a regular basis to strengthen your leadership strategies and commitment.

JIM KIM

As a physician and anthropologist, Dr. Jim Kim, CEO of the World Bank Group, has dedicated himself to international development for more than two decades, helping to improve the lives of under-served populations worldwide. In a recent discussion with Dr. Kim, he told us, "Every leader wants to find him or herself in a situation where people truly are able to check their own desires, their own personal needs at the door, and think about the needs of the organization as a whole, but it's hard. Ask yourself, if I really believe in my institution, what do I need to do to help it be as effective as it can be in accomplishing these great goals?" Dr. Kim believes that a commitment to growth and excellence is the creator of synergy. He concluded by adding that commitment is truly "trying to make a whole greater than the sum of its parts."

Notes:

_____

_____

_____

_____

_____

_____

_____

_____

_____

_____

_____

_____

_____

_____

_____

_____

_____

_____

_____

_____

_____

_____

_____

_____

READ HABITUALLY

The more that you read, the more things you will know.
The more that you learn, the more places you'll go. -Dr. Seuss

THE PLAY

Based on your value proposition outlined in the previous activity, it is time to read. No really, read. No, actually read. You are not speed reading this activity are you? In a world where everything comes to us chunked, tweeted, and bite-sized, you are losing your capacity to focus and to read. Reading is a lost art. The more brilliant the person, the more able they are to assimilate the knowledge and experience they have acquired and collected. When obtaining an advanced degree and writing a thesis, the first thing you have to learn to do is exhaustively research what is already available. You do not need to be quite as brilliant when you have diligently examined the existing wisdom. Your mobile device makes this information very easy to access. No excuses. Time to be better informed.

REQUIRED ACTION

Assess the current information that you have access to on a daily basis and think about the most recent book and articles you have read. Now answer the questions below to determine how you would describe yourself today.

What do you read on a daily basis?

_____
_____

How do you go about researching topics?

_____
_____
_____
_____

Are you knowledgeable in a well-rounded way? Business. Lifestyle. Sports. Front page news? What is the most recent book you have read?

_____
_____
_____
_____

How often do you Google the best sellers, fiction and non-fiction? Are you well versed?

_____
_____
_____
_____

What journals or books or information does your boss read? Where do you need to improve?

_____
_____
_____
_____

How can you create opportunity in your schedule for reading?

_____
_____
_____
_____

OUTCOME

Read for business. Read for pleasure. Subscribe to INC, Harvard Business Review, or your industry's publications. Be in the know to stay in the flow, and keep up on trends in your field and industry. Reading really partners nicely with a glass of red wine and an evening of relaxing. But sometimes, reading has to happen on the plane or on the go. Clearly you are committed to reading if you are completing this exercise. MVPs stay relevant. Update your knowledge.

ACTIVATE ACCOUNTABILITY

Accountability breeds response-ability. -Stephen Covey

THE PLAY

The most successful people fail more often than losers because they are always stretching themselves and others to reach higher ground. Losers are risk-adverse, more focused on not failing than on winning. Our research shows that people who have achieved anything worthwhile over the long term must have suffered many failed experiments on the path to lasting success. How can you harvest the tuition you have invested in that last mistake you made? You have paid dearly for it, so you deserve to take some benefit from the pain you endured. How can you turn your wounds into wisdom?

REQUIRED ACTION

Think of a mistake you have made over the past month that may have let down the organization or your team. How did you remedy that mistake? There are three steps to success:

1. Responsibility: How can you make it clear you are taking responsibility to get the situation fixed?

_____

_____

2. Reliability: How can you demonstrate that people can count on you to take responsibility in a consistent way?

_____

_____

3. Responsiveness: How can you respond faster next time? Our primal brain is driven in times of fear by fight or flight responses that are great for reacting to a saber-toothed tiger, but rarely useful for stressful situations in the office.

_____

_____

When people who feel you have wronged them have to wait for an answer, they assume the worst. Even if you do not have all the answers for the problem that has occurred, it is usually better to respond quickly with the information you have than to delay until it is all buttoned up.

OUTCOME

Imagine that you asked a loved one, "Do you love me?" and that person hesitated in even the slightest way. How would you feel? The longer you wait to do something about your mistake, the more others will feel you have violated their trust. Show credibility with responsiveness and action, and never be afraid to admit you do not know the answer right away. People do not expect you to be perfect, they expect you to respond quickly and make it right.

ELIZABETH SMITH

Elizabeth Smith is the Chairman of the Board and CEO of Bloomin' Brands. Since joining the company in 2009, her leadership has revitalized the organization, both within the United States and internationally. Smith said it is important for a leader to make mistakes and learn from them. A leader should be able to say, "I know that I don't know" and then actively listen. She also stated, "It is okay to make mistakes and fail but we've got to have the honesty and humility to call each other on it and move on." When she works with a new organization, she respects the existing culture, but also challenges the new. "I know that this organization has had a lot of success, and the world is now different. We will need to behave differently. But I won't rush towards, how people should behave." Instead, she believes leaders must create a bridge and "listen."

Notes:

_____

_____

_____

_____

_____

_____

_____

_____

_____

_____

_____

_____

_____

_____

_____

_____

_____

_____

_____

_____

_____

_____

_____

_____

EXCEED EXPECTATION

Do or do not. There is no try. -Yoda

THE PLAY

As you learned, accountability is important to develop trust with your team. Equally important is your ability to take advantage of opportunity, manage your commitments, and follow through. You never want to make a promise you cannot keep. It is also important to not turn down so many opportunities, as you will no longer be viewed as a resource. People like to feel they can rely on you and your leadership, so consistency is cherished more than charisma.

REQUIRED ACTION

When asked if you can do something, but you are not sure what to do or how to do it, what is your response?

_____

_____

When asked if you can do something, but may not have the time, what is your response?

_____

_____

The last time you committed to getting a project completed, were you able to meet or exceed expectations? If you could not do so, how did you deal with that situation?

_____

_____

How often do you decline opportunities? Why? What is the reason? Are you limiting your success?

_____

_____

OUTCOME

While most of us would prefer to be judged by our good intentions, people rarely understand intentions enough for evaluation. Outcomes and results define us. People will decide based on your accountability and delivery of expectations whether or not they can count on you. So when you make a promise to your team or colleagues, make it your top priority and take the steps necessary to deliver. Also remember to actively manage your workload in order to fully take advantage of opportunities that cross your path.

SIR KEN ROBINSON

"For most of us the problem isn't that we aim too high and fail - it's just the opposite - we aim too low and succeed," exclaimed Sir Kenneth Robinson. Sir Ken is an English author, speaker, and international advisor on education in the arts to government, non-profits, education, and arts bodies. He was Director of the Arts in Schools Project, Professor of Arts Education at the University of Warwick, and was knighted in 2003 for services to the arts. His TED Talks are some of the most highly watched and shared in the organization's history. Robinson believes in creativity and challenges the traditional methods of learning and organizational development. Robinson believes that exceeding expectation and seeking growth is a way to keep you engaged.

Notes:

_____

_____

_____

_____

_____

_____

_____

_____

_____

_____

_____

_____

_____

_____

_____

_____

_____

_____

_____

_____

_____

_____

_____

_____

TRANSLATE PERCEPTION

I'm fascinated by human behavior and by the worlds inside of people. -Johnny Depp

THE PLAY

It is hard to change and exceed expectations, if other people are harboring past perceptions. Do people really change behavior or is it just the perception that they have changed? Most of us see the façade or expectation that you have for others. If you believe someone is a bad listener, you will continue to watch for bad listening characteristics. It is actually easier for a person to change their behavior rather than **your** perception of their behavior.

REQUIRED ACTION

Think of a picture of a clock with Roman numerals on it. What does the "4" look like on that clock? If you thought of "IV," you are more than likely incorrect. In most instances, a clock uses "IIII" as the "4" on its face (see picture to right). Look at additional Roman numeral clocks to confirm.

The key to making real change happen is to be cognizant of the change you are making and following up with yourself on your progress. How can you effectively change your behavior or try to become a better leader or person?

_____

_____

_____

_____

If you are trying to change your negative attitude at work, and after six months of not saying anything negative, you put someone down in front of the team, most of them will walk away stating, *"He/She will never change."*

Take that same example, and say that you sit with some of your employees or your boss and you tell them, *"I'm trying to change this behavior."* Then, after two months of not doing the behavior you go back to them and state, *"I haven't been negative in two months. Do you have any feedback for me to help with the next two months?"* You do the same thing for the next six months, and then you say something negative. Now, when you go back for feedback, they will say, *"Just don't do that again. You are doing great."* The perception that you are trying to change is there.

OUTCOME

Involving your team in the process of your personal development will manage the perception of change. This allows your efforts in your personal development to flourish.

AICHA EVANS

When Aicha Evans entered Intel, she said there was a moment when she realized "everything that computes connects." This was a different way of looking at things. As corporate vice president and general manager of the Wireless Platform Research and Development Group at Intel, Aicha is responsible for driving wireless engineering for multi-comm products and Intel platforms, as well as emerging wireless technologies to lead this industry going forward. She noted, "Challenges excite me. Big challenges. The pitfall for me is finding ways to stay motivated. I have learned to have patience in the journey, to anticipate where things should go, to celebrate small successes and to find pleasure when things are moving. I like outcomes. On the other end, I want to sit on my porch at age 60 and say, I was part of making that happen." Take your own perceptions of the future, challenges or hardships and translate them into opportunity for growth.

Notes:

_____

_____

_____

_____

_____

_____

_____

_____

_____

_____

_____

_____

_____

_____

_____

_____

_____

_____

_____

INCREASE YOUR INFLUENCE

Connectors are people who link us up with the world ... people with a special gift for bringing the world together. -Malcolm Gladwell

THE PLAY

Once you fine-tune your leadership skills with the previous activities, you can begin to develop the ultimate leadership skill: influence. Influence is the ability to connect with others to achieve a desired result. Temporary influence can be garnered by an exceptional event, but long term, sustainable influence is built on getting it done on a strategic level consistently. Or as urban moguls rap, "all day e'ery day." On a personal level, influence allows you to fast track your career or your idea. As an MVP leader, you must have influence with work groups, the organization, and even the industry. It gives you the power to connect with people inside and outside your circle and impact situational outcomes.

In the following exercise, you will examine influence within your work environment and determine specific actions to increase your impact within the organization.

REQUIRED ACTION

Identify and define influence within your current environment. How does influence help you achieve your goals?

_____

_____

_____

_____

Where do you currently have influence? Evaluate why and how you have attained it.

_____

_____

_____

_____

Where / how do you need to improve?

_____

_____

_____

_____

Revisit the Communicate with Emotional Intelligence exercise. Describe your method of communication. Do you change your approach based upon the audience to increase your effectiveness?

_____

_____

_____

_____

What strategies do you employ for building rapport, networking, and building relationships?

_____

_____

_____

_____

What topic or discipline can build your contribution and intellectual capital to participate in a broader way, outside the organization?

_____

_____

_____

_____

OUTCOME

Leadership is driven by influence. Developing influence can help you achieve your goals. It will allow you to broaden relationships with your core team, it also will allow you to extend your reach and influence in the industry. Finally, it will help you to drive strategic initiatives based upon your expanded knowledge, network, and ability to get things done.

EXPAND YOUR NETWORK

*More business decisions occur over lunch and dinner than at any other time, yet
no MBA courses are given on the subject.* -Peter Drucker

The Play

Now that you have identified how you want to build influence, let's examine your network and opportunities to expand. Traditional networking puts too much emphasis on developing short-term contacts intended to meet your momentary needs and ambitions. Instead, you should consider what is better described as relationship management or community building. The key is to shift from transactional relationships to meaningful ones based on common interests and objectives.

Required Action

Consider your network of relationships, answer the following questions:

What professional organizations should you be a part of?

_____

_____

What organizations do your influencers (from previous exercise) and other mentors participate in?

_____

_____

_____

_____

What nonprofits contribute to your passions and professional interests?

_____

_____

_____

_____

Outcome

Strive for quality, not quantity, in your networking efforts. Networking can be overwhelming if you try to amass a certain number of people. Instead, select a few people to be in your network and invest in them. It is important to choose people who care about the same things you care about. These relationships will serve as your professional family; do not limit yourself when reaching out to new contacts. Be aware of your long-term goals; it may benefit you to begin networking with those who can help you achieve these goals set for five or ten years in the future.

INGRID VANDERVELDT

Ingrid Vanderveldt is a businesswoman, entrepreneur and investor who founded numerous business efforts, including *Empowering a Billion Women by 2020* and the Dell $100m credit fund. She is a member of the 2013 United Nations Global Entrepreneurship Council, inspiring leadership internationally. Vanderveldt also was named a Fast Company Super-Connector, creating value through social connections. We sat down with her to talk about the importance of building influence through networking. "Everything in life, but especially business, is based on relationships" Vanderveldt said. "If you build a network and connections, you will elevate yourself closer to the things you dream and desire to do." She believes that building relationships and a network are critical to leadership influence, and "influence is how you build exponential impact." Vanderveldt described the large Fortune 500 global institutions she works with and how they all want to do business with people who have strong networks, relationships and influence. "Working with a person of influence allows organizations to focus their energies, invest resources, and make an impact on a much larger scale."

Notes:

_____

_____

_____

_____

_____

_____

_____

_____

_____

_____

_____

_____

_____

_____

_____

_____

_____

_____

_____

_____

_____

_____

MANAGE YOUR DIGITAL AUTHENTICITY

Check yo self, before you wreck yo self. -Ice Cube

THE PLAY

So far in the Strategic MVP, you have discussed personal branding, igniting your passions, discovering your mojo, and outlining your ideal future. In this section, we highlighted several ways to personally develop. Now it is time to discuss HOW this all translates into your online presence, your digital brand, your electronic swagger, or your Klout score. What does the Internet say about you? What do you, via social media, say about you? Is this message in line with your goals and development?

In a world of complete connection, there are endless tools at your fingertips. The answer to any question is just a Google or a Wiki away. You can reach out to anyone, anywhere and research people, places, or things. This creates an environment of spectacular opportunity. This also can be horrifying if used inappropriately. As MVPs, you must actively manage your online personal brand just as carefully as your human persona. But remember to be authentic, have power over social media, and use it effectively to help you achieve your leadership goals.

REQUIRED ACTION

Tell your story in a way that represents your message. Being authentic requires creating loyalty and trust. It is okay to be vulnerable, but do not forget to check yourself along the way and manage the vulnerabilities so that they do not become liabilities.

Please Google yourself. What did you find? Any surprises?

_____

_____

_____

_____

Now Google your name with key words attached: Leadership, Success, Failure, Good, Bad. These word associations will help you to uncover different stories being told about you.

_____

_____

_____

_____

What are the key social media tools you use today? How often are they updated? What content do you share?

_____

_____

What message does this communicate?

_____

_____

List three key points that you want to emphasize in telling your online story.

_____

_____

_____

_____

How authentic do you appear, and is the message effective?

_____

_____

_____

_____

What changes need to be made? (Examine photos, sources, friends, blog postings, tweets, etc.)

_____

_____

_____

_____

OUTCOME

Recognize that being vulnerable and letting people see the real you is a way of establishing trust in others. Yet, leaders need to manage their message while understanding that everything can be accessed, copied, and used in or out of context. Living in a world "disconnected" from the internet is just not realistic. Use the web as a powerful resource to tell your story. But, do not forget to check yourself along the way.

SECTION III — HUMAN CAPITAL

When employees feel that the company takes their interest to heart, then the employees will take the company's interests to heart. -Dr. Noelle Nelson

Throughout the Strategic MVP book, we coached you through setting goals, visualizing the future, and making strides in your personal development. Now that the foundation is built, we will begin to discuss how to better develop the human capital you lead.

Ask yourself if you have the right team members, and if you were to add a person to the organization, what characteristics do you need from a candidate? This analysis will prepare you to recruit people to your organization who match your situation and the team culture.

Once you have the team in place, an important component to leadership is developing your team, asking questions, receiving feedback, sharing ideas, and empowering the people around you. We want to unleash your curiosity for leadership, innovation, and creativity.

Understanding what motivates, what drives, and what interests your team members the most will help you to really engage them in participating toward a common goal. Ask questions and listen to their perspectives so you can genuinely demonstrate an interest in their wisdom and insights. Jewels of information often arise from this collaboration, and the feeling that comes from being a part of the team or belonging to a community will increase the impact of the human capital you lead.

People are a valuable resource to the organization and to the bottom line. Investing in their development results in increased efficiency, job satisfaction, and financial results.

RECRUIT WITH ENTHUSIASM

Human Resources isn't a thing we do. It's the thing that runs our business. -Steve Wynn

THE PLAY

The rarest and most powerful skill of the individual leader is the ability to inspire others with enthusiasm and empowerment in times of competitive challenge and, at the same time, demonstrate the humility to listen, learn, and improve every day. Excitement for the future must outweigh the anxiety about change. So, how do you get great people to share enthusiasm and join the cause?

REQUIRED ACTION

Create your best-ever pitch to recruit the best people to come work for the company. Consider it an elevator speech in which you have 30 seconds to convince someone to come work for your organization. What would you say?

_____

_____

_____

_____

Take a look at what you described above. What are the five most important keys to success when convincing talent to come to your organization and stay?

1

2

3

4

5

Ask yourself, are you applying these principles to retain and motivate the team that is already here? Does everyone on your current team see growth and change as exciting?

_____

_____

OUTCOME

The best leaders are those who drive growth and do not let themselves get paralyzed by constant change and complexity. They get enough of the right people in the right seats to achieve their objectives, and to do that, they need to know how to sell employees on the mission of the organization. This exercise will help you consider how to be accountable for motivating and inspiring the best people and take full responsibility for creating a great place to work. The best people know the best people.

CHARLES SCHWAB

Charles Schwab is a businessman and investor who started his firm in 1971 as a traditional brokerage company and in 1974 became a pioneer in the discount brokerage business. Schwab believes his success is because of the business partners and friends he developed along the way. He said, "Nobody does anything worthwhile alone. The job of a leader is to recruit and develop partners." Mark Thompson spent a dozen years at Chuck Schwab's side. Schwab acknowledged, "I got through college with a lot of luck. I flunked English A twice at Stanford, which was tough for me because I knew I was smart. What I learned from that, though, has helped me be a better leader. Some brilliant entrepreneurs think they can do everything. But that's never true. The best thing I ever did was recognize my strengths and deficiencies. Then, at Schwab, I was able to build up great people in the areas of my deficiencies. Having a learning struggle early in life helped me recognize that."

Notes:

_____

_____

_____

_____

_____

_____

_____

_____

_____

_____

_____

_____

_____

_____

_____

_____

_____

_____

_____

_____

HIRE YOUR WEAKNESS

The smartest thing I ever did was to hire my weakness. -Sara Blakely

THE PLAY

When you know you are not a wizard in every subject, you are more likely to realize that the only way to build a team and organization is through and with the great talents and skills of other people who share your vision. That is the best trait any leader can develop early in his or her career. Hire your weakness.

REQUIRED ACTION

In the space provided, write down the things in your job that you do not like to do.

_____

_____

_____

_____

How can I help someone else develop a skill so they can help me?

_____

_____

_____

_____

How can I partner with people who would love to do what is necessary to get the job done?

_____

_____

_____

_____

_____

What actions are required to build a team to support me?

_____

_____

_____

_____

OUTCOME

In any organizational setting, the most respected, valued, and admired leaders achieve success only with the support and expertise of a great team. Sharing power and relying on others (especially when you think you could do it better) are often the most difficult skills for a person to learn. It is, however, the only way to build and scale a successful organization. No one does it alone.

JIM KOUZES

Jim Kouzes is a bestselling author, an award-winning speaker and, according to the Wall Street Journal, one of the best executive educators in the United States. Kouzes discussed the importance of collaboration and working with your team. "We often make leadership about the leader. In fact, it is not about the individual, it is about all of those individuals who have to work together collaboratively to reach very difficult goals." He discussed with us the importance of hiring your weakness - good people with complementary and synergistic skills. Kouzes continued, "One of the fundamental reasons why leaders get derailed along their path is because they forget this truth that you can't do it alone and think that they are the only individuals that count."

Notes:

_____

_____

_____

_____

_____

_____

_____

_____

_____

_____

_____

_____

_____

_____

_____

_____

_____

_____

_____

_____

_____

_____

_____

DETERMINE YOUR MVPS

*Where there is no guidance the people fall, but in
abundance of counselors there is victory.* -Proverbs 11:14

THE PLAY

As you know, MVP is an acronym for Most Valuable People. Part of your journey to become an MVP requires identifying the important people in your life as well. Who are your MVPs? Who are those individuals who make the biggest, most meaningful impact on both your work and your personal life? If you want to become essential, you must deliver value to these people and ensure they recognize that value.

REQUIRED ACTION

Write the name of every person you can think of who is essential to your life — both personally and professionally.

_____

_____

_____

_____

What roles do these people play in your success?

_____

_____

_____

_____

Who are other people you need to enroll as MVPs to become more successful in the future?

_____

_____

_____

_____

OUTCOME

Knowing your MVPs is one of the most important ways YOU can be valuable. Your people will pay close attention to the things that matter most to them, they will know if you are going through the motions or making a real effort to deliver on their biggest needs.

LISTEN AND LEARN

*It is literally true that you can succeed best and
quickest by helping others to succeed.* -Napoleon Hill

THE PLAY

Now that you have a list of MVPs in the previous exercise, what are you going to do with the information? How can you learn more about your team, support their dreams, help them to gain greater satisfaction and to achieve better results?

REQUIRED ACTION

It is time to get to know each of the people you identified a little better. Using the chart below, do your best to answer the questions listed about each of your people. If you do not know the answer, ask questions.

Name of MVP	Characteristics the MVP Admires	Key Roles the MVP Plays in Life (CEO, spouse, skier, volunteer, etc.)	Which Roles Does the MVP Love Doing Most?	What Does the MVP Complain About?	Hobbies or Interests of the MVP	MVP Expertise (What is the MVP good at?)

How can you help each person get more of what he or she values?

_____

_____

_____

_____

OUTCOME

Caution: Just because it may be important to you does not mean it is important to one of your MVPs. You need to learn to suspend judgment and see if there is a desire you both share. You may decide you cannot come to an understanding and must ultimately agree to disagree, but take a moment to determine if there is some deeper common ground from which you can both benefit over the long term.

Notes:

_____

_____

_____

_____

_____

_____

_____

_____

_____

_____

_____

_____

_____

_____

_____

_____

_____

_____

COACH THE UNCOACHABLES

The best thing you can say about any coach is that
his players play hard for him. -Terry Bradshaw

THE PLAY

Recognizing employees who are challenging is just as important as recognizing your star players. Even if you are the best coach in the world, some players and employees are uncoachable. Your traditional strategies are not going to work. It is difficult to understand, so you spend an extraordinary amount of time on the idea of changing these high-maintenance people, hoping they see the light, but it just does not happen. However, the good news is that the "uncoachables" are easy to spot, allowing you to move past and focus on the growing and forward-moving players.

REQUIRED ACTION

Think about each of your employees. Answer the following questions in the space provided:
Who do you spend a significant amount of time coaching, but there has been no change? What choices are they making regarding their future?

_____

_____

Do you have any employees who you believe are in the wrong job? If so, name them.

_____

_____

Do you have employees who think everyone else is the problem? If so, name them.

_____

_____

Do you have any employees who are pursuing the wrong strategy for the organization? If so, name them.

_____

_____

If you have any employees who fall into these categories, they may be considered to be uncoachable. The impact on the organization can be very detrimental as it diminishes your high-performance culture. It is time for you to examine whether these employees are a good fit for your team.

OUTCOME

When you have employees who are uncoachable, save time, skip the heroic measures - you will not win with these employees. Focus on the other players. There are times to coach a player, and there are times to coach them out of the organization. Make the adjustments quickly to allow you, your department, and your organization to move on.

EMPOWER YOUR PEOPLE

An ounce of performance is worth pounds of promise. -Mae West

THE PLAY

You have identified the important people in our life. You have identified those who deserve less attention or are uncoachable. You have also examined how you can build rapport and listen. Now let's take a closer look and examine ways to ensure that your people feel heard, valued, and understood.

REQUIRED ACTION

For this activity, select one person from your list on which to focus. This person should be involved in a current issue or project for which you are accountable. Then, in the space provided, answer the following questions dealing with that issue or project:

1. Purpose: What impact does he/she really want to have? How does he/she want to make a difference?

_____

_____

_____

_____

2. Passion: What personal interests or talents could he/she apply to this issue or project?

_____

_____

_____

_____

3. Performance: How will he/she measure short-term success today and every step along the timeline of this issue or project? How can I help him/her feel accomplished? How is his/her boss measuring performance?

_____

_____

_____

_____

OUTCOME

Use this activity for all of your MVPs you outlined in the previous activities. This is also very helpful to think about as you face challenges in new efforts or want additional involvement in change. When you understand a person's purpose, passion, and performance, you can unleash his/her efforts and foster growth and effectiveness.

RITA MCGRATH

Rita McGrath, a Professor at Columbia Business School, is a globally recognized expert on strategy in uncertain and volatile environments. She shared with us the importance of taking risks. "I actually have a concept I call learning from the intelligent failure, which really says that, in an uncertain environment, if you think about it, planning to be right is a fool's errand." McGrath believes that empowering your team to make decisions, to discover their passions, and to learn from failure leads to growth. Fostering intelligent failure is a measure of short-term success and speeds up the solution generation.

Notes:

_____

_____

_____

_____

_____

_____

_____

_____

_____

_____

_____

_____

_____

_____

_____

_____

_____

_____

_____

_____

_____

_____

_____

_____

MAKE VALUES VISIBLE

To win in the marketplace you must first win in the workplace. -Doug Conant, CEO of Campbell Soup

THE PLAY

Several companies have wasted millions of dollars and countless hours of employees' time agonizing over the wording of statements that are inscribed on plaques and hung on walls. There is a clear assumption that people's behavior will change because the pronouncements on plaques are inspirational or certain words integrate our strategy and values. There is an implicit hope that when people, especially managers, hear great words, they will start to exhibit great behavior. But this obsession with words belies one very large problem: There is almost no correlation between the words on the wall and the behavior of leaders.

REQUIRED ACTION

What are the values of your organization?

_____

_____

Engage with your employees about the followings questions. Write down their responses:
How have you (as the leader) modeled the values of the organization in the recent past?

_____

_____

How should a leader model the values of the organization?

_____

_____

What do you need to continue to do or change?

_____

_____

OUTCOME

Your actions will say much more to employees about your values and your leadership skills than words ever can. If actions are wise, no one will care if the words on the wall are not perfect. If actions are foolish, the wonderful words posted on the wall will only make the organization look puerile.

ALAN MULALLY

Alan Mulally is an engineer and highly successful business executive. He led Ford Motor Company through the crisis that rocked the U.S. auto industry while driving the organization's technological growth and innovation. Retired as Ford's President and CEO, Mulally was appointed to Google's Board of Directors. We sat down with Mulally to discuss his views on leadership. He passionately shared, "I really, really believe in the power of pulling everybody together around a compelling vision. Your biggest contribution as a leader is going to be: Holding yourself and your team accountable." Mulally has led thousands of people throughout his career, and he believes that a vision cannot be effective without knowing the organizational values and making a commitment to the people. Every leader must drive growth by "creating a comprehensive strategy and a relentless implementation plan with a management style that allows you to do it. It sounds easy. It sounds straightforward, but for the leader of whatever level, that might be the most important thing each of us does."

Notes:

_____

_____

_____

_____

_____

_____

_____

_____

_____

_____

_____

_____

_____

_____

_____

_____

_____

_____

_____

_____

_____

CHALLENGE THE UNETHICAL

One of the truest tests of integrity is its blunt refusal to be compromised. -Chinua Achebe

THE PLAY

If you are ever asked to do anything that you believe may be unethical, it is not only your right to express your concern - it is your responsibility. Many of the world's most highly-respected companies clearly communicate this guideline to all employees. Why is it that more organizations do not communicate this message? Leaders cannot pass the buck on ethical issues. All employees need to know that expressing ethical concerns is a key part of their job. It is never an option.

REQUIRED ACTION

Have you encountered a situation or been witness to unethical behavior? Please describe.

_____

_____

How can you clearly define the issue and prepare a case for your position?

_____

_____

When was the last time you challenged someone or something that did not seem right to you? How did it go? How did you go about challenging the issue?

_____

_____

Do you believe you have created a culture where your employees are comfortable challenging up (especially in terms of ethical issues)? Why or Why Not?

_____

_____

OUTCOME

The corporate scandals over the last several years have resulted in a lack of trust for major organizations. The conditions that led to ethics issues will not be fixed by having employees attend training programs or listen to motivational talks. Organizations that establish and implement clear processes for encouraging upward challenge can do a great deal to prevent problems involving ethics, integrity, and values. Trust is easy to lose and hard to regain. For many employees and for the public at large, it may take years of concerted effort to rebuild the credibility of large corporations. From both a business and a values perspective, it is worth it!

INNOVATE WITH AN ORGANIZATIONAL HOTBOX

The chief enemy of creativity is good sense. -Pablo Picasso

THE PLAY

Many of the most evolved leaders and innovative organizations conduct a version of the Organizational Hotbox: an open collaboration of creative people in a wildly limitless environment. Examples include the Facebook hackathons, Cirque du Soleil jam sessions, or as the rock band the Eagles described when they shot the cover of their self-titled album in 1972, "We just drove into the desert with a bag of trail mix, a bottle of tequila, and our music."

Creating strategy in a place of open collaboration not only can open the door to innovative solutions, it also can build a foundation for synergy and focus. How can you apply the concept of creativity, innovation, and research and development (R&D) in your leadership in a way that produces results? R&D is all about allocating time for innovation and thought leadership, team management from idea to execution, and requiring transformational leadership and elevations.

REQUIRED ACTION

How would creativity improve my leadership?

_____

_____

_____

_____

How could I facilitate an organizational hotbox at my organization? How can I make my people feel safe?

_____

_____

_____

_____

What incentives (intrinsic and extrinsic) can I provide to foster an environment of innovation and development with my team?

_____

_____

_____

_____

Which of my current contacts would provide value to my growth? Who should I be networking with to broaden my innovative perspective?

_____
_____
_____
_____

What cross-functional teams or multi-demographic committees could I create to enhance creativity in my organization or with my team?

_____
_____
_____
_____

OUTCOME

Creativity can be a valuable resource. Give your team enough space to develop solutions and build the trust in them to fully unleash their potential. Creating a culture of innovation and creativity begins with a forum where employees exchange freely and believe that anything is possible.

HOWARD MORGAN

Howard Morgan is venture capitalist, philanthropist, author, and contributing writer for Business Insider. He believes that leaders must have a voice and an outlet for creativity. Morgan shared, "One of the things that is not often talked about, that is highly undervalued, is having a point of view. And what I mean by that is, it is easier to have a point of view and be flexible around the fact that you could be wrong than it is to be ultimately aspired to the perfect answer before you take your first step." Leaders cannot be afraid to be creative and to make their voice heard. Organizations should work hard to unearth this creativity. "Take a look at some of the great technological minds we've seen and it's not that they've never made mistakes, it's that they keep driving at it."

DIVERSIFY OPINION

What is right is what is left if you do everything else wrong. -Robin Williams

THE PLAY

In addition to developing creative and innovative thinking, you also must encourage leaders to challenge the status quo and not be afraid to disagree with the consensus. Many leaders will say they want a team of independent thinkers, yet implement rules/policies/strategies that do not encourage this diversity in perspective. The synergy of your team comes from the strength of having multiple voices and perspectives to utilize.

REQUIRED ACTION

How do you encourage diversity of thought as you seek counsel and ideas from your team? Do you have a strategy to combat groupthink?

_____

_____

Do you assign a devil's advocate or contrarian in your meetings? If so, how does that work? If not, write down how you can execute this concept. It is important that the manager does not play the role of devil's advocate, because the team will assume you are not really interested in brainstorming.

_____

_____

How could you build this diversity/constructive-challenging behavior into your culture or organizational structure? For example, think about recruiting practices, incentives, or business partner relationships.

_____

_____

How could you reward the people around you to challenge the status quo?

_____

_____

OUTCOME

Being an effective leader means challenging the people around you to speak their minds. Leaders who foster an autocratic style and manage their employees' ideas will not be able to effectively innovate in the future. This close-minded approach is not adaptable enough to meet the ever-changing needs of the consumer and market. Give your employees a voice. Recognize that your team may need a little encouragement to speak up. Inspire creativity through outside the norm discussion.

URSULA BURNS

Ursula Burns is chairman and chief executive officer of Xerox, the world's leading enterprise for business process and document management. She has been instrumental in the evolution of Xerox from being a technology company to a services company that has significant influence globally. "I started with this approach that I have of, 'There's gotta be a better way.'" She started by looking at Xerox's basic business – managing the business process of communicating via page-based documents and instead of just perfecting that – and she did – and stopping there, she thought strategically. Ursula asked, "Why is it that we can break/fix, service and manage an office infrastructure with document technology for Xerox devices, but not everybody else's devices? It's the same device – so why can't we manage that infrastructure? Instead of having every business around the world do something that is inefficient, and therefore is something that they won't do very well, why not platform it?" Diversity of opinion on your team will help you to identify and challenge the status quo.

VINOD KHOSLA

Vinod Khosla is a billionaire businessman and a co-founder of Sun Microsystems, a company which created the Java programming language and Network File System. Khosla believes in the importance of speaking your mind and allowing your team to do the same. "Good CEOs should never really have to make a decision. Their team should know. They should be able to assemble a team that knows how to make all the decisions." He also noted that leadership takes courage and noted how easily influenced some executives can be. "CEOs are too influenced by what the public and the press has to say, reacting to a journalist who wrote an article in The New York Times or The Washington Post, Businessweek... They should not be reacting to the press. They should be **leading** the press. When the press disagrees, the leader should test the vision internally, get their team on what they're doing, and dare to disagree! It is amazing to me how many very senior CEOs don't have the courage to back their convictions. It is your job to have the courage of your convictions when what you believe diverges from conventional wisdom."

PRAISE PEOPLE

Outstanding leaders go out of their way to boost the esteem of their personnel. If people believe in themselves, it's amazing what they can accomplish. -Sam Walton

The Play

Actively looking for and pointing out legitimate examples of excellence in others is a tenet of leadership and makes you more valuable and admired. However, there is an art to praising others. When giving praise, make it real and authentic. Make sure you are specific about what others did well rather than making some general, patronizing statement about what a nice person they are.

Required Action

Take a moment to think about last week, and in the space provided below, write down everything that went well in your week.

_____

_____

Now, in the space provided, write down the names of all the people who helped you provide a positive outcome to your week.

_____

_____

Next, using "Thank You" cards or some other type of note card, draft an acknowledgement to those who were responsible for what went well this past week and include the following:

- What exactly they did
- What impact that behavior had on the overall mission
- What it meant to you personally

Deliver (in person or through the mail) each note to the individual you addressed within the next few days. Resist the urge to simply send an electronic message. Email will not have the same impact.

Outcome

It is important to state something specific when you are giving praise, as it will increase the genuineness of your comments and ensure the person feels valued for their contribution. Perceived mutual feelings of competence and confidence in each other will increase when you praise others in the workplace – and at home for that matter. Praise should become a best practice in any successful person's life – ensure you do so in some way each week, whether in the workplace or at home.

STOP AT GREAT

★★★

Our thinking and our behavior are always in anticipation of a response. -Deepak Chopra

THE PLAY

The higher up you go in your organization, the more you need to make other people winners and not make your job about winning yourself. The more successful you become, the more helping others win is how you win! For those in leadership positions, this means closely monitoring how you hand out encouragement and help others improve. If you find yourself saying, "That is great..." and then dropping the other shoe with a tempering, "BUT," stop yourself before you speak. Take a breath and ask yourself if what you are about to say is worth it. In most cases it is not. If you really want to succeed and encourage others to do the same, try stopping at "great!"

REQUIRED ACTION

The challenge for you this week is to not say "BUT" when you are listening to your direct reports or other co-workers. Every time you feel like you need to say, "That is great, but...," stop yourself at "great."

Write down how you felt each time this happened during the week in the space provided below.

_____
_____
_____
_____
_____
_____
_____
_____
_____

OUTCOME

A simple exercise in awareness of your language can make a great impact. Explaining why something will not work is different from adding value. "That is great, BUT..." can be used as a precursor to negativity or simply negate your previous positive affirmation. This exercise will help you pay attention to how you respond to your employees and help you become more positive in your approach with others.

SECTION IV — MAXIMIZING TIME

*This time, like all times, is a very good one, if we
but know what to do with it.* -Ralph Waldo Emerson

We have envisioned our future, set goals, empowered our team, and completed the necessary homework and learning. Now, we need to make it happen. Where will we find the time?

In the next section, we are going to ask you to conduct a quick evaluation of your normal day. What takes up most of your time? How much time do you spend on actual, productive work, and how much time is spent on putting out fires or distracting behaviors? Reflecting upon how you can commoditize and prioritize will be covered in this section. You will learn that checking items off of your to do list increases your energy and will give you a sense of accomplishment.

Balancing priorities and determining how to get things done in a more efficient way starts with a positive attitude. You may not always have the best circumstances, but you can always have the best intentions. When you consider a work week and think of how you might reconstruct your use of time, there are major implications on your success in both a professional and personal way. Just think, even 30 minutes per day redirected to work on a long term goal or an important project, will give you focus and a sense of achievement.

Time is our most valuable resource. Throughout the next section, we will examine time as a finite resource, helping to uncover efficiencies, deficiencies, and opportunities for maximization.

COMMODITIZE YOUR TIME

★★★★

I spend my time now buying time for the future. -Mark Perrett

THE PLAY

Let's begin our review of time by giving it the respect and authority it deserves. You should begin budgeting your time in the same manner that you budget money. As an executive, you allocate significant focus toward financial budgeting, investing, variance analysis, but rarely do you invest the same energy allocating our most prized resource, time.

How many of you have been to an ineffective meeting? How many of you went to one today? How many of you have read a book or been to a meeting on how to conduct more effective meetings? Life is full of energy-creators and energy-takers. What is important as an executive, MVP, is focusing your life and career on what you feel deserves this energy and time.

REQUIRED ACTION

Start by asking yourself; are there things in your life that you give yourself to (energy and time) that DO NOT deserve it? If so, what?

_____

_____

Next, what things in your life consistently need more attention that you rarely have time to give?

_____

_____

Finally, note the answers below in percentages. These three items should add up to 100%.

What percentage of your time is focused on activities that have a return on investment?   _____%

What percentage of your time is spent putting out fires?   _____%

Do you have time in your day that is wasted?   _____%

If you could eliminate one activity, what would it be? And how much time would it save you?

_____

What will you do with this extra time? _____

OUTCOME

Learning that time is a precious commodity may change your entire life. Each moment that you spend focusing on what matters most will help improve the quality of your life and your effectiveness in all aspects.

COMBAT MULTI-TASKING

F*cking two things up at the same time isn`t multi-tasking. -Dick Masterson

THE PLAY

Your effectiveness as a leader is largely determined by what you choose to do, and what you choose not to do, at any given moment. Knowing what to do and when to do it is vital to growth and success. Reflect on what you have learned so far throughout the Strategic MVP. Based on your personal development and growth, as well as your goals outlined in the previous sections, let's take a look at your task list for today.

REQUIRED ACTION

In the space below, write down your "Things to Do" list for TODAY. Prioritize this list by numbering each item using "1" as the most critical thing you must accomplish today.

THINGS TO DO TODAY:

1. _____
2. _____
3. _____
4. _____
5. _____
6. _____
7. _____
8. _____
9. _____
10. _____

What is your strategy to complete these tasks? How do you approach your day?

_____
_____
_____
_____
_____
_____
_____
_____

Are there things on this list that do not align with your goals? Are there things that you identified previously as undeserving energy-takers?

_____

_____

_____

_____

Do you believe you are smartest when you focus on one task at a time?

_____

_____

You should complete a variation of this activity every day. Trying to accomplish too many things at once hinders your ability to focus.

OUTCOME

As a leader, you have *too much* to do at any given time. Research also shows that 20 percent of your tasks will eventually account for 80 percent of your results; therefore, your ability to focus intensely on the most important results expected of you largely determines your success or failure in your position. Working single-mindedly on *the most important tasks* will help you accomplish two or three times as much as the average person.

CLIFF NASS

Cliff Nass was a professor at Stanford University, as well as an organizational development consultant who authored hundreds of papers and books relating to human-computer interaction and statistical methodology. Studies by Professor Nass confirmed that even exceptionally bright young people, who appear to be experts at multi-tasking among e-mail, instant messaging, and live communication, are not as accurate or effective in doing work as those who do one thing at a time. Nass recommended that leaders focus their energy on being great at one task at a time. He noted, "Many highly successful leaders are described as being intensely results-oriented. This results-orientation keeps them focused on a goal or task rather than sharing their attention amongst several things at once."

REDUCE INTERRUPTIONS

★★★★

There are always distractions if you allow them. -Tony La Russa

THE PLAY

Every time you stop a task and come back to it later you lose 5 to 15 minutes. It takes a while to figure out what you were doing and return to the mindset of accomplishing the task. This also happens to be the number one reason leaders make mistakes.

REQUIRED ACTION

Reexamine the action list you created in the previous exercise. If it has changed, please feel free to create a list of things you have to do for the rest of the week.

THINGS TO DO THIS WEEK:

1. _____
2. _____
3. _____
4. _____
5. _____
6. _____
7. _____
8. _____
9. _____
10. _____

Using the list above, circle three things that are the highest priority items. They should be items first on your list. Then, take a look at your calendar for the week. Block out time in your day right now where you can execute these tasks from start to finish.

Now, in the space provided, jot down ways you can minimize interruptions in your day while you work.

_____

_____

OUTCOME

When poet and author Maya Angelou wanted to be left alone to write, she rented a hotel room and told the staff that she did not want anyone to refresh towels or to turn down the bed. Most of us cannot afford that luxury. Coming up with your strategy will help you complete the things that you want and need to do each day.

DELEGATE

★★★★

*No person will make a great business who wants to do it
all himself or get all the credit.* -Andrew Carnegie

THE PLAY

There are a lot of things that only you are going to be able to do in your job; however, there are many things that you can delegate. Learning to delegate appropriately will be one of the most critical defensive strategies you can embrace as a leader.

REQUIRED ACTION

Who do you know that loves to do the task you dislike? _____

Can you automate any aspect of your work day? If so, how?

_____

_____

Can you eliminate any of the tasks you have during the day? If so, which ones?

_____

Can you double up on any of the tasks you have during the day? If so, which ones?

_____

_____

Can you use the Internet to help you run errands? (For example, can you grocery shop online and then just pick it up or have it delivered to you?) If so, what is your plan? _____

_____

Are there services in your area that pick up and drop off things you need (e.g., dry cleaning) so you can focus on what matters? If so, what is your plan? _____

_____

OUTCOME

Delegation will not only help you improve in your daily activities, but it will also help allow you to focus on what matters most and provide you with the ability to accomplish your goals. Remember when you learned about Hiring Your Weakness? This is a perfect example of where you place responsibilities upon those who will excel at the tasks that can be delegated amongst your team.

WRITE IN PENCIL

Transform your energy to flexibility and you will be free from what you fear. -Yoko Ono

The Play

One of the greatest challenges with time is the impact of change to our plans and actions. Have you ever been on the way out the door, when suddenly...your child lost a shoe...car is out of gas...unexpected traffic...boss calls an early meeting...who is parking in my spot?...where is my flash drive? In this world of lightning-speed change and ever-evolving leadership needs, have your budgets ever really equaled actuals? Have your plans ever gone off without a hitch? Rarely. Never.

Life is complex, requiring us to be flexible. Goal-setting is required as you force forward into the future, yet flexibility allows us the opportunity to dance in the face of change. When you write in pencil, you can erase.

Required Action

What areas of your life need more flexibility? Please list your ideas below.

_____

_____

Is your day so structured that it does not allow time for a deep breath or an unexpected issue? If so, what can you do to adjust the schedule?

_____

_____

What type of item on your to-do list or calendar constantly gets moved? What can you do about it?

_____

_____

Who is available to support you when things change? _____

Outcome

One of the most important leadership qualities is flexibility. This is as true for you as an individual as it is in business. The more flexible you are, the more you remain open-minded regarding the various ways that a sales or a business goal may be achieved. Remember to prepare for flexibility and accrue for change. It is important that you, as a MVP leader, are clear about the goal or project, but flexible about the process of achieving it. If you allow for flexibility in your budget, you will make room for growth and evolution.

MAYA HU-CHAN

Maya Hu-Chan is an international management consultant, executive coach, author, and sought-after speaker. She is rated as one of the Top 100 Thought Leaders by *Leadership Excellence Magazine* and Top Leadership Guru from Asia by *Leadership Guru International*. Hu-Chan shared, "You have to be able to adapt, you have to be able to stay open and to continue to be curious and ask questions and learn about people, learn about different markets and learn about cultures and then reflect on what does this mean and how do I personally need to change and adapt so that I can be more effective?" This approach to leadership allows continual growth and flexibility. Adaptability is required in the fast-paced business environment.

Notes:

_____

_____

_____

_____

_____

_____

_____

_____

_____

_____

_____

_____

_____

_____

_____

_____

_____

_____

_____

_____

_____

BE PROACTIVE

If you don't know where you are going, any road
will get you there. -Cheshire Cat, Alice in Wonderland

THE PLAY

Wait. Are you worrying about yesterday's issues? There will always be crises that must be managed, but the difference between being proactive rather than reactive is making the time to really decide where you want to lead your organization. Bill Gates shared with us, "How will you help others solve problems to build a better future? Don't obsess about the past. You have to learn from your problems, but stay focused on the road ahead, not just what is in the rearview mirror."

This activity is meant as a self-check. How are you doing in this moment? This exercise can be used from time to time to remind yourself how effectively you are proactively seeking growth.

REQUIRED ACTION

Review your Commoditize your Time, Combat Multi-tasking, Reduce Interruptions, and Delegate exercises. Take a look at how you manage your time and schedule. Review your upcoming week and schedule. Then answer the following questions:

What percentage of your time is focused on proactive activities? _____%

What percentage of time is focused on the goals you outlined in Section I? _____%

How much time would you like to be focusing on proactive growth? _____%

How does this proactive preparation benefit the organization, the clients, and yourself?

_____

_____

_____

_____

_____

_____

OUTCOME

Your clients are counting on you and your team. When they provide you with their hard-earned time and money to do business with you, they are looking for you to help them be better. What are you creating that is bigger than you are? By being proactive, you anticipate and prepare to add value to your clients and you become invaluable to the organization. When you change your point of reference from a reactive mode and all the distractions to a more specific, organized approach, it allows you to become a MVP and plan for the future.

MAKE TEMPORARY SACRIFICES

The secret of getting things done is to act! -Dante

THE PLAY

Even if you properly manage your time, combat multi-tasking, and maintain your flexibility, there are still a myriad of things to accomplish. When you are trying to maintain your focus on getting things done, you, as an MVP, may need to make temporary sacrifices.

REQUIRED ACTION

In the space provided, write down everything that kept you from accomplishing what you wanted to do yesterday. Be specific.

_____

_____

_____

_____

Now, reflect back to the exercise about commoditizing your time. What things are time-wasters throughout your day?

_____

_____

_____

_____

What are your lower priority items that can wait another day to free up time for priorities?

_____

_____

Now, take a look at the lists and circle at least one or two things you will NOT do TODAY so you will be able to accomplish your tasks.

OUTCOME

Simplify the best you can, but do not add to your list of things to do without taking something off your plate. Making temporary sacrifices is both identifying things that take up too much of your time as well as understanding your priorities so intimately, you can manage urgencies.

DE-CLUTTER

*The more you have, the more you are occupied. The less you
have, the more you are free.* -Mother Teresa

The Play

Cluttered workspaces can clutter your mind and be distracting. Many of our closets, garages, and cabinets are bursting at the seams. Some people have a hard time throwing things out that do not relate to their current goals because they worry that those things might support a future passion. Do you keep unnecessary files? Is your desk so cluttered you cannot focus?

Required Action

Take a look at your office. How does it appear to others?

_____

_____

What can I do to my office to create a work space that maximizes productivity?

_____

_____

Is my office reflective of my personal brand?

_____

_____

Take a look at your home. List some areas within your home that you can de-clutter and make more efficient:

_____

_____

Spend some time today finding a place where you can stash anything *not* related to your current goals. It can be a safe, a storage unit, a file cabinet, or whatever you think will work to keep you focused on what matters now and not on something that distracts you. If possible, do not just merely stash these items, but rather discard/shred/recycle anything unnecessary. Free your mind!

Outcome

Keeping your focus on what matters most is critical to your future success. Keeping those things that distract you out of your view will help you stay true to what you need to accomplish right now. Remember your previous exercises where you determined your goals. This exercise will help you to reduce interruptions and focus on what matters most for you to achieve what you need to achieve.

SECTION V – EXECUTING STRATEGIES

*I've always considered myself to be average. What I have is a
ridiculous, insane obsessiveness for practice and preparation.* -Will Smith

Section V will allow you to anchor the changes you made while reading the book and to develop new standards of success. Creating new benchmarks for your leadership development will institutionalize your new, revisited, and refreshed approaches into the culture of your organization, allowing you to enjoy and benefit from the fruits of your labor.

Strategic thinking has an important role in establishing business practices and creating a foundation for the long term success of an organization. However, executing on strategic initiatives separates the MVPs from the other leaders within the organization. We all have encountered people who talk a great story, but have limited impact on the organization's success. It is the people who can work with others, manage projects, and make initiatives happen that will drive their own future and create passion within the team.

As a MVP leader you must exemplify the culture you expect and model the way. Reflect upon your approach to each day, each employee, and each task and bring your super hero, humble mentality to the work environment. It will build confidence in you as a leader and also give your team an example to follow. You will also increase your job satisfaction in knowing that you have contributed to a job well done!

Section V will reveal tools to help you let go of frustration, recognize the necessary commitment, leave baggage behind, and free yourself to capture the next opportunity.

REMOVE THE UNNECESSARY

I'm starting with the Man in the Mirror, I'm asking him to change his ways. -Michael Jackson

THE PLAY

Many of the smartest people in business do not ever fully succeed because they get in their own way. You need to find ways to use rationality to increase output, not hold you back. Have you ever created your own roadblocks keeping you from success? Think about what those roadblocks were and why they held you back. Today, you are going to start your extreme makeover. This means you need to REMOVE all of the things from your life that are inconsistent with your passions and goals.

REQUIRED ACTION

Take a moment and make a list of those things that are **not in alignment with your passions and goals**. Make a list of all the things you identified throughout the Strategic MVP book, including time-wasters, ineffective policies, low priority goals, old perceptions, inappropriate digital social media content, etc. Do not limit yourself. Write as quickly as you can.

_____

_____

_____

_____

Based on this list above, what must you STOP doing?

_____

_____

_____

_____

What will you START doing differently today?

_____

_____

_____

_____

OUTCOME

Everything you bring into your life either supports or undermines who you are and what you want to create. There is a famous saying, you are what you surround yourself with. Choose wisely. If you have negative and discouraging influences around you, then ultimately that is who you will become. Surround yourself with friendly, driven, and encouraging influences that positively affect who you are.

IDENTIFY WHO IS STANDING ON YOUR CAPE

God sent me on earth to do something and nobody can stop me. -Bob Marley

THE PLAY

You are going to continue removing the unnecessary things that are not in alignment with your passions and goals from the previous exercise. Now, let's focus on the PEOPLE in your life (including yourself) who may be holding you back. Be honest about your relationships and think about strategies to eliminate the people who are standing on your cape.

REQUIRED ACTION

Do you have people doubting you or holding you back? If so, who and why?

_____

_____

How can you eliminate their voice?

_____

_____

Do you have people supporting you in your development? If so, who and why?

_____

_____

As you begin to implement the ideas presented throughout this book, where have you identified that your confidence is lacking?

_____

_____

Where are you the most confident? How could you apply this energy to the above?

_____

_____

OUTCOME

At this point in your journey, it is all about execution and making things happen. In the popular animated hit, *The Incredibles*, the brilliant costume designer, Edna Mode, lamented the many times capes got caught on things and created unnecessary accidents for superheroes. Her advice: No capes! If someone is standing on yours, it is hard to take flight with your leadership skills to make a difference – personally and professionally.

SHERYL SANDBERG

Activist, author, and technology executive, Sheryl Sandberg is an American icon who has driven the issues of gender equality and women in leadership to the forefront of industry. She argues that in order for change to happen, women need to break down these societal and personal barriers by striving for and achieving leadership roles. The ultimate goal is to encourage women to lean in to positions of leadership because she asserts that by having more female voices in positions of power, there will be more equitable opportunities created for everyone. Sheryl is the Chief Operating Officer of Facebook and is the first woman to serve on Facebook's Board of Directors. She once said, "We can each define ambition and progress for ourselves. The goal is to work toward a world where expectations are not set by the stereotypes that hold us back, but by our personal passion, talents and interests." Sheryl urges women to not let others or themselves get in their way to achieving their aspirations.

Notes:

_____

_____

_____

_____

_____

_____

_____

_____

_____

_____

_____

_____

_____

_____

_____

_____

_____

_____

_____

_____

_____

SMILE

The purpose of our lives is to be happy. -Dalai Lama

THE PLAY

Humor makes it a whole lot easier for you to accept who you are and what happens to you. If you can laugh at adversity and enjoy this kind of rough-and-tumble learning in your personal life and work, you will enjoy the journey much more. It is equally important to stop and enjoy the celebratory and amazing moments along the way.

REQUIRED ACTION

Think about the last time something did not go quite the way you anticipated or a time when things went horribly wrong. Were you able to laugh at yourself? If not, why?

_____

_____

What tools can you use to help you find the humor or even something positive in the midst of a storm?

_____

_____

What area of your life needs more laughter and smiles?

_____

_____

How can you create that energy?

_____

_____

OUTCOME

Many successful people face lifelong adversity or flaws they never overcome – but they do find a way to manage them. They refuse to let their goals and dreams be held ransom by their feelings in that awful moment when everything has gone wrong. When you can laugh at your faults, your optimism shines through! When you understand mistakes happen, and you can learn from them with a smile or a laugh, others around you will focus on the take-away from the situation rather than the negative outcome.

MARTHA REITMAN

Martha Reitman, M.D. is CEO of Reitman Corporation, a company providing worldwide strategic development support to companies developing novel therapeutics and devices for the treatment of human disorders. She believes that the mind impacts the body more than leaders realize. "The hurt is there and to pretend that it is not isn't healthy," said Reitman, talking about her own journey. Enjoying life and smiling can be a good remedy to the stress of executive work. "You're going to be in shock for a while...Acknowledging that is critically important if you're going to deal with it." This acknowledgement of impact is critical to make the appropriate steps forward. "That's when you can start to get solace from the doing. You can rebuild, you can make use of this – and that's very affirming," she said. Life is a precious journey; you can take care of yourself with something as easy as smiling. Laughing is even better!

Notes:

BLAST TARGETS

Why have you not broken from the pack? You're playing it safe?
Safe ain't gonna get you sh!t in this world. -Stone Cold Steve Austin

THE PLAY

Live today as if it is your last. Live life to the fullest. YOLO (you only live once). There are endless clichés describing the importance of living full out. Blasting targets is the concept of demolishing goals and entering your leadership journey with a strong focus. If in fact, you only have one opportunity to live today, what are you doing to make things happen?

But sometimes, even the most highly successful athletes and executives have caught themselves making excuses with stories like...*I haven't had my coffee...I'm not a morning person...I've got kids...I'm bad at math... It's not my job...I'm not good enough...*Today, this whining ends. Do not just hit your targets, growth, and goals – BLAST them.

REQUIRED ACTION

If today was the last day you had in your current position, what would you do right now?

_____

_____

If today were the last day as you know it (major change or devastation on the horizon), what would you stop and be thankful for right now?

_____

Who in your life deserves more attention? How can you dedicate time to that relationship right now?

_____

_____

If you could change how you spend the day, while still working toward your goals as you outlined previously, how would you?

_____

_____

OUTCOME

It is often said that as we near the end of our career there are reflections on what was missed – regrets of a lifetime unfinished. Living life in the moment is much better than reflecting upon the past or longing for the future. No more coulda and woulda for you. You are an MVP.

BECOME THE MVP: BLAST TARGETS CONTINUED

Charge 'em brah! -Fellow surfer encouraging the next wave

THE PLAY

Based on the previous exercise, now it is time to continue that Blast Targets mentality and...integrate the philosophy into your daily routine. A can-do attitude begins before your alarm goes off and continues throughout the day. You recognize that the difference between ordinary and extraordinary is just one little word, extra! Blast it. Your energy will attract other high performers who have a desire to get more from every day.

REQUIRED ACTION

Think about the last time you blasted targets, accomplished a goal, or totally kicked butt in your life... What does that MVP rockstar in you look like? Where does that person show up? Describe.

_____

_____

What leadership characteristics did you emulate? Name 5 characteristics of your Blasting Targets inner MVP:

1
2
3
4
5

What impact does your inner MVP have on others? Are you creating an energy that permeates your environment?

_____

_____

_____

_____

Think about the opposite side of you - the person that has insecurities or lacks confidence. The person who is afraid of failure. What characteristics does this person have? What areas of life does this person show up?

_____

_____

_____

_____

Now, think about how your kick-butt, inner MVP can help you to obliterate the insecure person described above. They are both within you! How can you apply the Blasting Targets MVP characteristics to your goals and intentions you have set throughout this book?

_____

_____

_____

_____

OUTCOME

The Blast Targets exercise, applied personally and professionally, will leave your best on the field of play. Today is an opportunity for you to blast your targets. Rise up, see the goal, and go for it. You will spend your career and your life full engaged. What more is there? Demand greatness from those around you and from yourself. Play full out. Be an MVP!

Notes:

_____

_____

_____

_____

_____

_____

_____

_____

_____

_____

_____

_____

_____

_____

_____

_____

_____

_____

_____

_____

_____

REFRESH YOUR SWOT

You gotta wanna, because no one else will wanna for ya. -Ken Blanchard

The Play

Excellent job. Your personal SWOT was the first exercise you completed to identify your baseline - your strengths, weaknesses, opportunities, and threats. Throughout the book, you examined this assessment in depth to uncover dormant talents and strengths, to help you capitalize on opportunity, and to build on weaknesses.

Required Action

Please revisit your initial SWOT and reflect on the following questions.

Strengths: What steps are you taking to increase your strengths? What areas have you improved during this journey?

_____

_____

_____

Weaknesses: What strategies are you employing to build upon your weaknesses?

_____

_____

_____

Opportunities: Have additional opportunities surfaced? Have you dedicated time to seeking opportunity?

_____

_____

_____

Threats: Have your leadership threats evolved? What threats are still imminent?

_____

_____

_____

Outcome

Reflecting on your initial intentions and goals helps to reflect the growth in the journey. Your leadership evolution requires, and will continue to require, active effort and action.

SUMMARY

The question isn't who is going to let me; it's who is going to stop me. -Ayn Rand

Congratulations! You have completed the Strategic MVP and the exercises recommended by top coaches and executives from around the globe. We hope you are inspired to live full out and reach your destination. Enjoy this moment and feel proud of your growth and accomplishment…But your work is not done!

This Strategic MVP book required you to dig deep and to engage in the process to fulfill your potential and create action. You completed 52 exercises, utilizing the tools of top executives and highly successful people, learning some incredible approaches on what to start doing as well as what to stop doing. Now, we want you to continue to interact with this book for it to have lasting value: share it with your team, reflect on what you have learned, and execute your strategies.

Many of the exercises in this book were focused on personal growth – while others stretched your leadership skills when guiding a team. Now, follow up with the teams you lead and use the Strategic MVP as a tool to enhance their skills. Sharing and communicating knowledge is often a greater challenge than possessing knowledge. Share your growth and lead your team through their development. Being an MVP requires developing others around you to excel.

We also challenge you to review your work, reflect on your learnings, and refresh your action as needed. You, as the MVP, will have to continue to adapt. Stay open and be curious, ask questions and learn about people. Absorb and reflect on the knowledge and ask yourself, "How do I personally need to change so that I can be more effective?"

Finally, we have delivered strategies to you, coaching you through the process, creating a forum to generate ideas. And we all know, **ideas alone are not enough**. It is great to read books, study, and listen to the most powerful and highly successful people. But, when you finish a book or lecture, what have you really learned? We believe that **applying** the skills and tools and **executing** the strategies is the key to success. We need you, MVP, to spread the buzz, to stimulate growth, and to exemplify change. We challenge you to arouse your followers, your organization, and your industry. The real MVPs implement the ideas and knowledge through doing. Take your exercises, coaching tips, and tools and **apply them in your life today**.

APPENDIX

ACHIEVE

GOAL: _____

PRIORITY #

What is the measurement?

_____
_____
_____
_____

What is my deadline to achieve this goal?

_____
_____
_____
_____

What will I need to do to accomplish this goal?

1
2
3
4
5

When am I going to start this goal?

_____
_____
_____
_____

How will I keep this goal in the forefront so I will remember to focus on it every day?

_____
_____
_____
_____

ACHIEVE

GOAL: _____

PRIORITY #

What is the measurement?

_____
_____
_____
_____

What is my deadline to achieve this goal?

_____
_____
_____
_____

What will I need to do to accomplish this goal?

1
2
3
4
5

When am I going to start this goal?

_____
_____
_____
_____

How will I keep this goal in the forefront so I will remember to focus on it every day?

_____
_____
_____
_____

ACHIEVE

GOAL: _____

PRIORITY #

What is the measurement?

_____
_____
_____
_____

What is my deadline to achieve this goal?

_____
_____
_____
_____

What will I need to do to accomplish this goal?

1
2
3
4
5

When am I going to start this goal?

_____
_____
_____
_____

How will I keep this goal in the forefront so I will remember to focus on it every day?

_____
_____
_____
_____

ACHIEVE

GOAL: _____

PRIORITY #

What is the measurement?

_____
_____
_____
_____

What is my deadline to achieve this goal?

_____
_____
_____
_____

What will I need to do to accomplish this goal?

1
2
3
4
5

When am I going to start this goal?

_____
_____
_____
_____

How will I keep this goal in the forefront so I will remember to focus on it every day?

_____
_____
_____
_____

ACHIEVE

GOAL: _____

PRIORITY #

What is the measurement?

_____
_____
_____
_____

What is my deadline to achieve this goal?

_____
_____
_____
_____

What will I need to do to accomplish this goal?

   1

   2

   3

   4

   5

When am I going to start this goal?

_____
_____
_____
_____

How will I keep this goal in the forefront so I will remember to focus on it every day?

_____
_____
_____
_____

ACHIEVE

GOAL: _____

PRIORITY #

What is the measurement?

_____
_____
_____
_____

What is my deadline to achieve this goal?

_____
_____
_____
_____

What will I need to do to accomplish this goal?

1
2
3
4
5

When am I going to start this goal?

_____
_____
_____
_____

How will I keep this goal in the forefront so I will remember to focus on it every day?

_____
_____
_____
_____

ACHIEVE

GOAL: _____

PRIORITY #

What is the measurement?

_____
_____
_____
_____

What is my deadline to achieve this goal?

_____
_____
_____
_____

What will I need to do to accomplish this goal?

1
2
3
4
5

When am I going to start this goal?

_____
_____
_____
_____

How will I keep this goal in the forefront so I will remember to focus on it every day?

_____
_____
_____
_____

ACHIEVE

GOAL: _____

PRIORITY #

What is the measurement?

_____
_____
_____
_____

What is my deadline to achieve this goal?

_____
_____
_____
_____

What will I need to do to accomplish this goal?

    1
    2
    3
    4
    5

When am I going to start this goal?

_____
_____
_____
_____

How will I keep this goal in the forefront so I will remember to focus on it every day?

_____
_____
_____
_____

AUTHOR BIOGRAPHIES

MARK C. THOMPSON

Based in Silicon Valley, Mark is a senior executive leadership coach, a successful business leader, New York Times bestselling author, venture capitalist, and Tony-nominated Broadway producer - and brings real-time solutions to today's leadership challenges.

Mark is Charles Schwab's former Chief of Staff, Chief Customer Experience Officer, Chief Communications Officer, and cofounder of the Schwab Foundation. He served as the Executive Producer of Schwab.com, with assets of over $3 Trillion. Forbes Magazine called Mark one of "America's top investors with the 'Midas' touch." Mark was cofounder of Virgin Unite Mentors, Sir Richard Branson's network for executive coaching and entrepreneurial innovation, and is a Founding Patron of Virgin Unite's Entrepreneurship Centres. Mark was also Program Chairman for the Board of Governors of the Hesselbein Leadership Institute and the John F. Kennedy Institute for Entrepreneurial Leadership.

He is a founding advisor of the Stanford Realtime Venture Design Lab and a visiting scholar at his alma mater, Stanford University. He has served as faculty at the World Economic Forum and the World Business Forum. He is a SupporTED coach on the team that coaches TED Fellows.

Mark served on the Board of Directors of Best Buy, Korn Ferry, and Interwoven (now owned by HP). He was Chairman of Rioport – which popularized the MP3 player prior to the iPod and iTunes - and was Chairman of Integration, which was acquired by Silicon Labs.

He is a Founding Board Member of Smule, which is Google and Apple's top music applications company - including a top selling app for the hit TV series Glee - with over 60 million active users. He is an investor in Cancer Genetics, a leader in DNA-based cancer diagnostics for personalized clinical management of cancer treatment.

Among his passions is Broadway. As a producer, Mark's plays have earned five Tony Awards and ten nominations, including Peter and the StarCatcher with Disney, and StickFly with Alicia Keys.

Mark lives in the San Francisco Bay Area and in Manhattan with two extraordinary women – his wife Bonita and their daughter Vanessa.

BRANDI STANKOVIC

Dr. Brandi Stankovic is an organizational change consultant and a motivational speaker with a creative, people-centric and results-driven approach to problem solving and planning. She is a founder and senior partner of Mitchell Stankovic and Associates (MSA), a global strategic consulting firm. She has more than 15 years of experience in providing solutions for clients, including award-winning education, strategic planning, leadership transition, and human capital management. Brandi spends her time consulting with CEOs and their teams, writing books and articles related to leadership and organizational health, and speaking to audiences from around the globe.

Brandi inspires audiences with her models of leadership, organizational culture, and employee engagement. She is a top-rate keynote speaker who utilizes humor, story-telling, and a dynamic and interactive style to leave audiences feeling energized and ready for action! Brandi is the author of hundreds of whitepapers and journals as well as two scholastic publications: *Business Performance Measurement, Intellectual Capital Valuation Models* and *Social Media Strategies to Advance Organizational Change*.

Prior to MSA, Brandi worked as the Vice President of Marketing and Administration for Ventura County Credit Union and also as the Director of Education at Harland-Clarke, a Fortune 500 Company serving financial institutions.

Brandi is the Young Leaders vice chair for Children's Miracle Network Hospitals Credit Unions for Kids, the Human Resource Development Network Board consultant, World Council of Credit Union's Global Women Leadership Network sister society advisor USA, volunteer manager at Aid for AIDS Nevada, and an International Development Educator CUDE and I-CUDE.

Brandi is an adjunct faculty member at the College of Southern Nevada, comprehensive exam faculty reviewer for Pepperdine doctoral candidates, and is certified in teaching English as a foreign language. She received her Bachelors in Finance and Economics at the University of Nevada, MBA from the University of San Diego, and Doctorate of Education in Organizational Leadership from Pepperdine University.

FOREWORD AND CONTRIBUTING AUTHOR

MARSHALL GOLDSMITH

Dr. Marshall Goldsmith has been recognized again as one of the top ten Most-Influential Business Thinkers in the World and the top-ranked executive coach at the 2013 biennial Thinkers50 ceremony in London. Dr. Goldsmith is the author or editor of 34 books, which have sold over two million copies, have been translated into 30 languages, and have become bestsellers in 12 countries. He has written two New York Times bestsellers, *MOJO* and *What Got You Here Won't Get You There* – a Wall Street Journal #1 business book and winner of the Harold Longman Award for Business Book of the Year.

Marshall's global professional acknowledgments include: Harvard Business Review – World's #1 Leadership Thinker, Institute for Management Studies – Lifetime Achievement Award (one of only two ever awarded), American Management Association - 50 great thinkers and leaders who have influenced the field of management over the past 80 years, BusinessWeek – 50 great leaders in America, Wall Street Journal – top ten executive educators, Forbes – five most-respected executive coaches, Leadership Excellence – top ten thinkers on leadership, Economic Times (India) – top CEO coaches, Harvard Business Review (Poland) – Leadership Thinker of the Decade, CEO Global (Canada) – World's #1 Leadership Speaker, Economist (UK) – most credible executive advisors in the new era of business, National Academy of Human Resources – Fellow of the Academy (America's top HR award), World HRD Congress – global leader in HR thinking, Tata Award (India) for Global HR Excellence, Fast Company – America's preeminent executive coach and Leader to Leader Institute – Leader of the Future Award. His work has been recognized by nearly every professional organization in his field.

Dr. Goldsmith's Ph.D. is from UCLA's Anderson School of Management, where he was recognized as the Distinguished Alumnus of the Year. He teaches executive education at Dartmouth's Tuck School of Business. He is one of a select few executive advisors who have been asked to work with over 150 major CEOs and their management teams. He served on the Board of the Peter Drucker Foundation for ten years. He has been a volunteer teacher for US Army Generals, Navy Admirals, Girl Scout executives, International and American Red Cross leaders – where he was a National Volunteer of the Year.

35410682R00071

Made in the USA
San Bernardino, CA
23 June 2016